I Can:

Succeed At My Job

By: W.L.W. Borowiecki

To all those people I've worked with over the years: I've learned a lot from all of you and maybe, just maybe I can do my part in passing on some of the things you taught me. And also for our three sons, Wilbur, Luke, and Watson.

Contents

Foreword

In my case, I worked for over 40 years at various jobs, from manual labor to engineering design to working with shop floor mechanics on how to assemble parts. I've worked both in union-represented jobs and supervisory positions. I've worked detached special assignments where I've been tasked with "here's a situation so go figure out if there's a way it can be made better". I've met and worked with thousands of people from janitors to the chairman of the board, presidents, and vice-presidents. (I even shook hands with a former US President, but that was a non-work occasion.) I recently retired from a job I held for the last 36 years. I know that long of a tenure in one job is unheard of with today's generation of workers, but that's what I think is the easiest way to get ahead in your business without burning bridges behind you.

I'm a fairly straightforward person, I usually say what I mean, and I usually do what I say I'm going to do. I can work with just about anyone but there are people that have not been able to work with me because I usually take a business-first attitude while I am at work. On the other hand, if it allows me to get my job done faster or easier, I will be only too happy to listen to how your pet schnauzer has the runs and you have to get new carpeting installed.

For at least the last 15-20 years I was the top ranked engineer in my job category with a big title and a generous paycheck. Some people in my office would express awe at my very official sounding title, but I would tell them not to think of me as some superman able to leap over tall buildings with a single bound, but rather just a demigod able to leap over two stacked shoe boxes on one of my good days. I've had great experiences and some downright ego-smashing bad experiences that left me wondering why I was even born. I've met great people that I hope to remain in contact with for the rest of my life, and met a few other people that I'd like to meet in a dark alley sometime and let them know what I really think of them. Along the line, I've coached and mentored many people of which some later became outstanding employees in their own right.

One final point about me now that you're thinking I am one of the most reactionary, regressive, boring, stick-in-the-mud old fuddy-duddies you've heard of in a long time. I have been told by quite a few people I've worked with over the years that I have a very good sense of humor (a case in point when one manager in a meeting I was in was lamenting about "how are we going to get this done?" to which I immediately replied "with a swish and flick" with which most of the people present burst out into laughter). One of the last comments I was told before I retired was "I've always appreciated and will miss your wicked sense of humor". That means just as much to me as being able to look back on a successful working career.

So now that you're fairly impressed with my credentials and viewpoint, let's get down to business and let me coach you on how you can become a productive person in your business, and more than that, how to be the person that others including the management staff will rely on. That in turn will get you better ratings and hopefully more cold hard cash in your paycheck.

Side Note: Read the companion to this book titled "I Can: Be A Great Manager" for ways to take the next step and become a good if not great manager with topics such as Dealing with Your Manager, The Downside of Management, Leading Your People, and Is It All Worth It?

Why am I working?

Nobody likes to work. Those people that say "I love my job" or "I love to work" say so because their job allows them to do what they want or like to do, *and* get paid for it. If given a choice between going to work five days a week or staying at home and being able to go out fishing, skydiving, snowmobiling, or whatever one wanted to do while getting paid the same amount, how many people would choose to go to work? Probably a whole lot less than the amount of people currently employed. Priests do not love to work; they love the opportunity to lead people in developing and showing inner faith. Police and fire fighting personnel do not love to work; they want the opportunity to lead and protect their communities by giving them a sense of security through enforcement of laws and protection from man-made or natural disasters. The President of the United States does not love to work; he has a vision of how life should be and feels the need to lead others in achieving his vision. I did not like to work, rather I liked the chance my various assignments gave me to solve puzzles and fix problems.

So let's get a few things straight right off the bat. I am going to address that work is work. Work is not the social hour. Work is not where you find your next partner or spouse. Work is not happy hour without the alcohol. Work is producing something your employer wants, needs, and values, whether it be flipping 147 burgers per hour or designing a new propeller for nuclear submarines. I once had a newer employee tell me that he wished he could bring in his football because he thought he could relax and think better if he could occasionally toss that old pigskin around the office. My reaction was initially unprintable but I think I eventually managed to blurt out something like "that's really idiotic, and besides what happens when you bean the office administrator in the head and send her to medical?" Really folks, leave fun and games out of it and just let work be work. Work is difficult enough to accomplish without bringing in other activities. It's best to concentrate on the work at hand and leave the humor to occur spontaneously, besides it's actually more fun that way.

One caveat to what I'm going to go over and explain to you is these guidelines worked for me but they may not work for you. I am not going to guarantee immediate world-smashing success for you but I will say that listening and heeding at least some of what I say is going to make you a better employee able to work more productively, and for your part it should lighten some of the stress you may be feeling in trying to make a success of your career. So the net result is a win-win situation for you and your company; the company gets a more productive worker and you get a better chance at the fame, responsibility, and pay you feel you deserve.

Let's start at the very beginning with the most basic question of all. Ask a dozen people why they work and you'll get at least two dozen different answers but the most common reasons why people work boil down to the following three in order of frequency:

To pay the bills / buy what I want

To raise the kids properly

To make a difference

Just like all those other millions of workers out there, I never really wanted to work. I wanted to sit around all day and do what I wanted whether it was being a slug in front of the tv all day, reading books, or whatever. I didn't want to expend any energy unless it was something I really wanted to do like racing go-karts or playing softball with the other kids on the block. My parents had an entirely different view based on their life experiences which were honed in the first half of the 20th century (they grew up during the Great Depression). Their basic concept was "you're not getting anywhere sitting on your butt all day". To them, 'getting anywhere' was synonymous with being successful at some job where the income earned was enough to pay for essentials like a roof over your head, food to eat, and a bed to sleep in (they were very basic people). My aspirations eventually were a bit more than that however. I wanted all those things they wouldn't buy me, like a new bicycle. Well, through their tutelage I soon found out that if it was worth having, it was worth working for. (By the way, my grandmother finally got tired of me whining about that bicycle and forked over the cash for it.) So I had assigned jobs around the house during the week and as a result I can say that over time I developed some pretty good bathroom cleaning skills.

Now ask yourself why you work. Examine what you want out of life, then start researching how much that is going to cost in terms of dollars, energy, and time. So you want that new 450 horsepower supercharged car that can go from zero to sixty miles per hour in under four seconds, well how much is that going to cost to buy or lease? Forty thousand dollars? More? How much is that going to cost for insurance? Fifteen hundred a year? More?

That's why we all work for a living, to get what we want out of life whether it's material things or inner satisfaction. In any case, there is going to be a price to pay for those things. If I decide that I want to make a difference by organizing people against unfair laws, that is a noble reason but unless I'm independently wealthy, it won't do much towards keeping a roof over my head or food in my stomach. If I decided I wanted to make a difference by becoming a grade school teacher, yes I can keep a roof over my head and food in my stomach but there's an awful lot more that I'm going to have to give in terms of personal time and energy to make that difference.

You have to decide why you're working and what effort that is going to require. If you are looking only to keep some clothes on your back and some food in your stomach as you take a year to hike from San Francisco to Boston, that means that you're not going to have to be very picky about the jobs you take along the way. You're also not going to be **able** to be very picky about what jobs you are offered. If, on the other hand, you have four kids at home that's a good reason to get a fairly steady dependable job that you can count on to supply a reasonably steady income. If you're looking only to buying that turbocharged supercar maybe that will result in a part time job or working some extra overtime?

Whatever your reasons for working, compare your desire to what the requirements of the desired job are. That is going to be a large part of the decision on which jobs you will or can take. If your inner passion is to be a yoga teacher but you have an elderly penniless parent to care for, maybe being a yoga teacher full time is not the job for you, part time maybe but I don't think it's going to pay your and your parent's bills by itself.

Examining the reasons why you are working is the first step towards being successful and more importantly, being happy with your life. There are people who are very successful but are not that happy with their life and vice versa. I once worked with a person who had started working for that company four days after I was born, and here he was, 26 years later still doing the same job as when he hired in. He was happy, he was content, and in his mind he was successful. Other people saw him as a person who shirked responsibility because he had refused multiple promotions, but he wasn't working for promotions, he was working for the sake of working. He found a job he was good at, he performed well, and he went home every evening knowing that he accomplished what he set out to during the work day.

So ask yourself "why do I need to work?" and "what do I expect to get out of this?". Then take a look at what your job is and do the comparison – does this job fulfill my requirements? If you have children at home and you are the sole income source, it's doubtful that a job working at the local car wash is going to fulfill the need of being able to support those children. Then what do you do? Put forth the effort and look for another job of course. Don't just sit there and say "there isn't anything else out there so I have to stay here". That is a cop-out to yourself and to your dependents; it is a statement that you have given up. There is always something else out there although you have to put forth the effort to find it, nobody is going to drop it in your lap.

From unemployed welfare scammers to people that develop smart phone applications and make millions, these people all put forth some effort necessary to make their living. If you don't foolproof your smartphone application program, it's going to get tagged as worthless and nobody will download it, so you have to put effort into making it work correctly. Even the welfare scammer has to work at filling out all those forms and going through all the motions necessary to get that monthly paycheck, they just don't call it working for a living. Those people may be considered slugs by others because "all they do is sit on their a$$ all day long". But is that a reason for you to do the same? Do you really consider their lives successful? They aren't really living an easy life either because that welfare check doesn't do a whole lot towards putting the kids through school or getting that supercar you always wanted. Yes, you can have a 'successful' life with an illegal career but there is a price to pay; a couple years in jail, ruined credit, or people perhaps out for your blood. It's a lot easier and safer to try and be successful with a more traditional career.

So what's the reason why you work? Take that and mesh it with what work you want to do and see what comes of it. Is it possible that you could take a lower paying job that would be enormously more satisfying and still satisfy why you need to work? Do you need to get a higher paying job or just something part time to tide you over that new motorcycle purchase?

Summary Point:

Why do you need to work? Answer that and you've taken the first step to becoming a success.

What is a work ethic and what does success mean to me?

To summarize the various definitions available from different sources, the term 'work ethic' says that work is both intrinsically valuable and it also strengthens moral character. It is not the same as ethical work which I would define as some variation of labor that produces morally acceptable results. That is a moving target based on the person's learned values and general societal values. I am going to go over what work means and what it should mean to you if you have any dreams of achieving some success in your career.

So what is your work ethic style? Are you driven to get all your assignments done as quickly as possible, or do you enjoy being able to multitask so you can keep your fingers in many pies, or something completely different?

To answer this question, you should first off realize that your personal work ethic is comprised of many parts, two major pieces being: what you enjoy or are interested in, and the other is the underlying reason or reasons why you are working.

So the part of your answer about enjoyment or interest is rooted in why you chose to accept this job or work in this field. If you are like most people, you chose a field that you liked and or were somewhat good at in school. But don't think that something you like but couldn't really get the hang of doing means that you are going to have to settle for something less than your aspirations. You may also find that as time goes by you find something else that interests you more. I worked with a lot of people that did not have engineering degrees or backgrounds that were quite happy with working in an engineering department. I've worked with other people that had engineering degrees that sooner or later ended up working in Sales and Marketing or other non-engineering departments. Those people's ideas of success obviously changed over time. Or, on the other hand, you may find that although you've always really wanted to be an airline pilot but you just don't have the skills and patience to be one. There are other associated jobs out there in the aviation world where you could use that desire to be successful with airplanes such as air traffic controller or airplane mechanic.

Don't be panicky or depressed because your life's dream appears either unachievable or just not what you thought it would be. Be resilient and look to revise your life's goals as you gain experiences, more in the next chapter.

I always wanted to be an architect from the time I got my first little log kit to play with as a child. I wanted to design buildings but when I got into architecture school at college, I soon found out I really didn't have the vision or more importantly the talent necessary. I transferred into Civil Engineering because it was close to architecture in that CE's build things, and that's really what I wanted to do. One of the CE classes I took was on designing structures to withstand various loads and involved figuring out how many bolts or rivets to use to connect together steel beams and columns. I was really really good at that and got an A in that class, but I hated it to high heaven.

So, after two years in college I was at a depressing point. I was in a field that was my second choice, finding out that I especially hated designing structures, something that had been my childhood dream. That was a rude wake-up call for me to re-examine my life goals and my plans for becoming the success that I, and more importantly at that time, my parents wanted. I can still hear my mother telling me "the world needs good ditch diggers" when I came home with less than stellar grades for the second year in a row. At the time, I thought she was telling me that if I didn't get that education all I would be good for was digging ditches. Much later in life I came to realize that what she was really telling me was that no matter what I chose to do, I should exert all effort possible to do whatever 'it' was well, and to the best of my abilities.

And that is what I am talking about when someone asks me about 'work ethic'. *It is doing your utmost to succeed in whichever job role you've chosen or been placed into.*

In my case, what I ended up doing for 30 plus years may not have been what I originally wanted to do or thought I wanted to do, but I worked hard at it and succeeded. Would I have rather been designing buildings? Looking back on my life since beginning college I would have to say 'no'. What I chose to do with my career turned out to be at least as enjoyable and fulfilling as I think designing buildings would have been. I made a choice of careers and because of my work ethic I made my career which in turn fulfilled my ambitions for success. If I had chosen a different career I think my work ethic would have still brought me success, and of course a completely different life than the one I've lived for the past umpteen years. So the adage "work is what you make of it" rings true for me.

Choosing a career based on what you want to do and what you think you're good at has a bearing on how successful you are going to be, but it's not everything. You may be one of those people that say "I'm not good at math so I can't be an engineer". That's an incorrect perception on your part. A neighbor's daughter had expressed an opinion once about wanting to be an engineer but later on said that she couldn't do that because she wasn't good with numbers. Knowing how to manipulate numbers does give one a step up in the engineering field but it is by no means all of it. It is similar with other fields of study. To be a doctor or pharmacist requires knowledge of chemistry and biology which in turn also requires some skill with numbers but again it's not the whole thing. There's a whole lot more to a chosen field than just the technical data, besides with the explosion of the internet a very large part of the technical data and pertinent equations is readily available in any given field if you know where to look. What I'm trying to get across is that to succeed in a field, one must throw away a lot of those preconceptions and just get in there and do it.

Ok so you've chosen a field of work and are in your entry level or later job. Now what are you going to do? My advice is to continue developing your work ethic. In high school or college, you started developing your adult work ethic and whether that was three hours of study every night and then hit the bed, or it was study for an hour, hit the local club, then stumble into bed a couple hours later, it was your work ethic that you were developing. If you're like me and the countless millions of other people like me, you get up in the morning, go to work, spend ten or more hours in traveling and time on the job, then home for something to eat, some quiet time reading or watching television, then hit the bed for the night. On evenings and weekends throw in some housework such as laundry, vacuuming the carpets, taking the kids to soccer practice, lawn mowing, etc., and then start over the next week. In all this, work-work and house-work, you are further refining your work ethic. At home, you see a job that has to get done and some people do it without much thought at all (while others have their partners 'remind' them). At work, you are given assignments and you are expected to complete them satisfactorily. In both cases, there are things that need to get done and completed satisfactorily. There's really not that much difference between house-work and work-work once you reduce it to this basic state.

As I mentioned, I have had various different job assignments in my life and for each one of them, I did as well as I could for the most part. The manual labor jobs I held, well those just required me to show up, get a certain amount of stuff from here to there, and then punch the time clock. I could have worked faster I suppose but it would not have made any difference in the overall scheme of the company I was working for since I was mainly working on a fixed speed conveyor line. But at least I paid attention and didn't screw up or off. The office jobs I've held required me to actually think about what I was doing and since I can be a pretty lazy guy at times, I spent a lot of that thinking time wondering how to make my jobs easier to accomplish. These attributes, paying attention, willingness to do what had to be done, and thinking of newer and easier ways, made me stand out after a year or two as someone who could be trusted with more leeway and more freedom to act. In this I was inadvertently helped by some of the other people in my office. A few of the other people in my office weren't there to work; they only wanted to collect a paycheck and that's what set me apart from them. There was that one person that piled books all around the edge of their desk and set their chair as low as possible so that no one would see when they either dozed off or were doing non-work stuff at their desk. Another person spent a fair amount of time cruising up and down the aisles stopping here and there to chat with someone else and not really accomplishing any assignments. There was even one person that spent a fair amount of time during the work day trying to get people interested in his idea of investing in diamonds. I don't know if these people considered themselves successful in the life they were living and the work that they were doing, but to my eyes they were wasting opportunities to be at least more successful.

So if you haven't gotten the message yet it's this: Do whatever you have been assigned to do and do it as well as you can. That is the work ethic that will get you noticed and gradually more freedom to do the job the way you think and want it to be done. At one point in my career, the work group I was in was running a series of those infamous three and five day workshops

17

for groups of cross-functional people. We usually had food delivered which meant that at least once a week we were getting pizza delivered. My boss decided after the second botched delivery that someone should instead go and pick it up so I volunteered. It was a job; it had to be done, and most importantly got me out of the boss's view for a while. Plus, it was a chance to show that I was willing to do what it takes to get the job done. It may have been a coincidence but after two months of those workshops and me delivering pizza once or twice a week, I started getting higher-grade assignments and the boss began asking for my opinion on matters. I had demonstrated my determination to get done what had to be done and was recognized for it.

In terms of success, my definition is I think fairly modest and one that anyone can understand. I never needed to be the boss, I didn't need to make a million dollars a month, and I didn't need the rest of the department to bow and kneel as I walked past. There are quite a few people that I've met over the years that I think firmly believe the above criteria is the true definition of success but I'm not buying into it. Success is coming home after work and saying to the mirror "I made a difference today". *If you can't find at least one instance during the day where you found the answer, solved the problem, finished the project as well as you could, found some new piece of information you didn't know before, or just plain helped someone else out, you're either not paying enough attention or you are not doing your job.*

Final words on work ethic. Work ethic is not complete without the underlying drive or passion that drives the development and implementation of your work ethic. I hesitate to use the word 'passion' in this case because there's countless other works out there that explain how to work with passion. I am not speaking of being a cheerleader that is constantly exhorting others to work faster or smarter because it's the job and everyone should just be doing their best because it's the end-all to be-all. I am speaking of segregating your feelings for the job or company you're working at from your feelings to perform the job you've been assigned to do. I worked at one company that I really didn't care for or respect a whole lot, but I had a job to do and I did it well. I didn't do this job well for the company's sake; I did it for my sake and my inner peace of mind. So your passion for doing a good job does not have to be connected to the company you are working for. You can have a butt-head for a boss but that doesn't mean you have to sacrifice your inner peace because of it. Enjoy what you are doing because you are doing it well and just ignore the rest of it; you will sleep easier at night.

Summary Point:

To put it bluntly, develop your own work ethic around doing the job at hand, doing it well, and quit grousing about how crappy your job is. It may not be what you originally planned to do or wanted to do, but at least it feeds the bulldog, and there may be ways to work around your current job assignment.

If you really don't like what you're doing, read the next chapter on careers, goal setting, and plans.

Setting my goals and plans to get there

Goals encourage us, spur us into motion, and give us reasons for our life. If goals are only random thoughts in your mind, they don't have the meaning and influence over your behavior that they should. Goals are those future states that we aspire to reach and unless you figure out how to set reasonable, achievable goals you will always be disheartened and soon take on the attitude of "why bother?". You don't need to set a goal for your entire life (although it helps), but rather the setting of several, or a sequence of, shorter term goals will help you see your near future more clearly, will help you in achieving a series of personal victories, and will allow you to branch out or pursue alternate paths and goals as you progress through life instead of locking yourself into that one path to your life's goal.

Everybody from my parents, teachers, and bosses always seemed to be asking "what are your goals in life?" throughout my life to this point (my wife continues to ask me "what are your plans for retirement?" so the questions never really end). Everyone has their own unique set of goals, and thoughts on how to get there. For the longest time I had the goal of winning a lottery and 'being able to finally do what I want'. Winning the lottery hasn't happened but for the most part I've still been able to do what I wanted to do, so maybe this is a case of just one goal not necessarily leading to your desired state of living; there may be many routes and goals that can provide what you really want. The goal is the destination and the route you can take is the plan to achieve your goal, but along the route you're traveling there may be forced and voluntary detours that may affect where you wind up at the end. Therefore, goals must constantly be evaluated and mid-course corrections be just as constantly implemented. You go to the grocery store with the goal of finding something for tonight's dinner. You may have a taste for something but if it isn't there, priced too high, or something else looks more appetizing, you do a mid-course correction and pick that something else up. You have just revised your goal and that's what you also need to do with your career on a regular basis, examine and revise as necessary.

Your career is going to be based on your goals and plans of action so you need to realize something very important about your career. Let's say you come into a new work situation and start to meet the people. Chances are that you will meet people that are so ambitious that they don't pay attention to anything other than their own ambition. When you first meet one of them, the conversation usually goes something like this:

"Hi, my name is Celine. I just started working here in the accounting department doing accounts receivable."

"How do you do Sybil. I'm Mr. Awesome and I can tell you that all your efforts are appreciated in keeping this company running. What do you think of this company?"

"My name is CELINE. I just started and haven't done anything… "

"Well that's just fine Sybil. I can tell you that this place would be a nightmare if I wasn't around to keep fixing things. What do you think of this office?"

"CELINE!! Like I said, I wanted to…"

"Hey Sybil, it was great talking to you but I have to run again, there's always something that blows up on a regular basis around here. See you later sometime. Keep up the good work."

And you will run into people like this sooner or later, guaranteed. They may not be as pompous as I've portrayed above, but they will not really care at all about you or your career, unless you are in a position above them. More about how to work with these and other people later on.

So who really is in charge of your career? The easiest and best answer is YOU. You may end up blaming your boss for not giving you that promotion or raise, but ultimately the reason that you didn't get that promotion or raise is within you. That's probably the most painful realization that you'll ever make in life, that *what happens to you in the workplace is the direct result of who you are and how you interact with others*. It's as easy as; if you and your boss don't mesh very well you're not going to be at the top of the promotion list. How do you rectify that situation? Examine how you work and how that intersects with what the boss is expecting of you. You don't know what the boss expects of you? Ask. It's really just that simple.

But it ultimately always comes down to you. I've worked for managers that were real butt-heads but I still took the time and energy to at least ask what they wanted and expected from me. I worked for one person that absolutely refused to tell me how well I was performing, even on the official end of year written performance review. I repeatedly asked for quality comments and just as repeatedly got nothing more than a condensed version of my job assignments. I realized that I had two paths to follow at that point; I could go sulk in the corner and let my morale sink another notch, or I could figure out a way to get a real performance review on paper. I took the latter path and went to the Human Resources person for my department and asked for clarification on whether or not actual performance comments should be included in my review. That answer was yes as I knew it was going to be. Now to that point in my career I had never rocked the boat at all so it was a surprise that the very next morning the department manager called me in and asked me to shut the door, always that most terrifying of all office procedures. The manager then surprised me and told me about reviewing my boss's comments and how they were sorely lacking on performance or quality comments and how the manager decided to add his comments as to how well I was actually doing. I was taken completely by surprise and extremely grateful for the manager's efforts. The manager also made some comments to me directed at my boss about "fixing his a$$" and called my boss to his office after sending me out. The same scenario as with me ensued with the door shutting but when the door opened again, my boss was quite red in the face and hurriedly scurried back to his desk. I looked out of the corner of my eye at the manager and he just smiled, nodded in my direction, then went back into his office. From that point on, the department manager would occasionally drop by my desk to 'see how things are going' and I got very good work reviews from then on.

Now without me doing something about my own career, would anything have happened? No, that bland piece of paper would have been filed away, the department manager would not have recognized yet another young capable employee, and it's quite possible that a year later when I was being considered for layoff, that I would not have survived the labor cuts as in fact I did. So take charge of your own career because nobody else is going to do it for you. And how do you take charge of your career? Set some goals and make some plans.

So what are your goals in life and in work? Nobody can set them for you so you must set them yourself. I attended a weeklong seminar on goal setting once where the general drift was that you can achieve any goal you set if you plan to reach it and then follow your plan. I was a bit underwhelmed by this seminar since it really seemed a no-brainer to me and to sit day after day with 25 other people who just ate it up didn't sit well with me. One of the very basic problems I had was with the presenter's main point of "you can achieve anything if you follow your plan to get there". Nowhere was there mention of outside influences, like the one manager I really liked that had a heart attack, was out for 5 months, and as a result I ended up working for someone else who was a complete pig-head. In the seminar, I remember I got into a bit of trouble with the moderator by commenting "so I decide that I am going to have the world's most perfect teeth. I clean and floss multiple times per day per my plan. I go to the dentist one morning for a checkup and get hit by a semi-truck and half my teeth get knocked out. Where is the influence of the rest of the world taken into account in regards to 'you can achieve anything'?" The moderators didn't want to hear that at all and as a result later on in the seminar I got paired up with another skeptic for a special project which wasn't all that pleasant. After that seminar I also ran up against my immediate boss's beliefs in that seminar's teachings. I got less than my usual stellar ratings in my annual performance review because my boss felt that I was not stretching myself in relation to my already demonstrated capabilities and intelligence. When I showed some confusion on this, the boss went on to explain that a person of my talents and experience should be setting goals mostly based around ascending the management ladder, because that was what *her* definition of success was. Well, my response of "I'm not that ambitious, I just want to do a good job" didn't go over very well at all and I got lower than average marks as a result. My boss and I continued to not mesh well on this point and the next two years or so were a bit of a chore for me to 'prove' that I was doing more worthwhile work than what was written on that piece of paper.

Having some goals in your work-life is going to make going to work that much more bearable and to some extent enjoyable. But a note of caution from experience is be smart about it. Let me relate a completely true story about a 'goal' I once talked about. A long time ago I was working in an office that was run by a second level manager that had a reputation for being a very hard-nosed, authoritarian person. It was on the eve of my five-year anniversary and I was tied up in a very lengthy project that involved a lot of paperwork to keep track of when my immediate boss gave me a form to fill out with my name, age, outside interests, and so forth. I asked what it was for and he told me it was a cheat sheet for the big boss so he could have an informed conversation with me in his office while giving me my service award. Being fairly young at that time, I was more interested in getting that project done than sitting with this fearsome manager for 20 or 30 minutes. I knew that that manager didn't really care about me and was just looking to check off one more thing that he had to get done. The next morning, I went into the manager's office along with two other people also getting service awards. The manager had a short conversation with each of the other people then eventually turned to me and asked how I liked working for the company for the last five years and did I have any plans for the future with the company. While he was asking me this I saw his eyes move down to his open desk drawer and there was enough hesitation in his question that I knew he was reading from the form I had filled out. That made me a bit angry that he didn't even know the people that worked for him so I then did the absolute stupidest thing that I've ever done in my life. If I did this in today's workplace, I'm sure I would be forcibly escorted out by security. I looked this fearsome manager in the eye and blurted out "well I was thinking of assassinating you and taking over your job". His jaw dropped, the other two recipients stared at me with that look that said "you're a dead person", and my immediate boss turned bone-white as if I had just insulted God. Thank goodness there was another first line manager there with a good sense of humor who started laughing so hard his face literally turned purple. All this happened in a split second and then the big bad manager also started laughing. He finally paused long enough to choke out "whoa there, I've only got a couple years left so give me a chance to retire". A few minutes later we broke up and as I was walking out of the office, the laughing manager managed to stop long enough to slap me on the back and tell me that was the funniest thing he'd heard in a long time. But then my immediate boss grabbed me, pulled me aside, and proceeded to tell me in no uncertain terms if I ever did or said anything like that again he would personally make the rest of my career a hell on earth, to which I agreed that this was an extraordinarily stupid career ending thing that I had just done.

But you know what? That manager that I had just insulted took to liking me because I stood up to him and either didn't cower in his presence nor toady up to him (like my immediate boss). After that whenever he was walking around the office, he'd often stop at my desk to just ask "how's things going?". To this day, I maintain that his big bad exterior was just a role he played so that he could order people to do things without getting any backtalk. If anyone ever asks me about this story, I will swear on whatever authority you want, or take a lie-detector test because it is all true. My advice to you is to remember this stupidity on my part with the goal of never doing anything like it yourself. Be smart about your goals and don't be an a$$ like I was.

Goals will fall into different categories and as a result, should get different priorities assigned to them or you'll be wasting your time working on them. Goals can be classified as must-do, should-do, can-do, and want-to-do. An example of a must-do goal is finding a way to provide shelter and food for yourself and your dependents. An example of should-do could be you find a way to care for an ailing parent or reporting a car-pedestrian accident. A simple can-do goal can be something that you already know how to do but just haven't gotten around to yet. Those goals that you want-to-do are things you've always wished to do but haven't the foggiest idea how to do, like skydiving for instance. Look at your goals and see where they fall, then categorize them to assign a priority to them. It does no good to spend a lot of time and energy to figure out what you want to do and see when you eventually get around to going to Italy sometime in the far future while ignoring how you are going to pay next month's rent.

So how do you set career goals? I've found that setting a career goal or goals requires that one has to break down desired job titles and assignments to a more basic level. If I go through the help wanted ads in the newspaper I don't only look at job titles but also job descriptions. Then I compare those descriptions to my qualifications and experience, and also to what I want out of the job. Let's go back to wanting to be an airline pilot. The training and education are readily available at various schools so achieving an entry level job shouldn't be that difficult to qualify for. So the question of do I apply for this job comes down to how does it fit in with my desires and requirements for a job? If I say I desire a job that lets me meet new people every day, allows me to travel to different cities, and allows me a degree of

25

freedom in accomplishing the job; wouldn't being a long-haul bus driver also fulfill my desires? Might being a long-haul bus driver be a very much easier job to attain seeing as how the training and educational requirements are much less stringent than for an airline pilot? So what I'm getting at is you have to break your goal down into your personal needs and desires, and then start re-assembling the components in various ways to come up with your career goals. If you put your needs and desires together *this* way you may find that being a schoolteacher would fulfill your goals whereas if you put them together *that* way you wind up with being a short-order cook as a goal. If you're an introvert like me, do you really want to apply for a job as a car salesperson? You won't be happy with that decision until and unless you can modify your own personal traits which in turn are the most basic drivers of your desires and wants.

So you're one of those people that say "I hate doing 'x' but I'm going to force myself to get good at it because I want to stretch and better myself"? That attitude of going against your inner nature in setting your goals as a way of developing or improving yourself takes an awful lot of willpower and willingness to repeatedly fail in order to accomplish, and I wish you well in your endeavor. You may be able to do it, you may not, but that is what life is about – new experiences.

You'll have to go through some self-evaluation if you want to set your goals so that they don't conflict with your inner nature to any great extent, and also to satisfy those inner desires you have. Think of it this way; you absolutely love chocolate ice cream and don't care a whole lot for strawberry ice cream. You go over to your friend's place for dinner and dessert is a special treat, strawberry ice cream. Now that strawberry ice cream is ok; it's dessert; your host likes it; and it does kind of finish off the dinner but it's not your favorite. Eating chocolate ice cream would have satisfied you a whole lot more because it is something you really enjoy; the strawberry ice cream was a bit of a let-down. It's the same with goals. *If you set a goal that isn't really in line with your inner desires and inclinations, you're not going to be as satisfied when you achieve that goal.* So to achieve the most satisfaction you either change your goals to align with your inner self or you find a way to change your inner self to match a goal. That's how people who set goals outside of their inner capabilities, desires, and needs (or comfort zones) decrease the fear associated with reaching for those goals that scare them.

How do I explain this without using advanced goal-setting theory? Let's try geometric terms instead. Say you want to drive from Dallas to Chicago but that's not going to work for you because you have to go through Missouri where you have fourteen outstanding traffic tickets, so you're always putting off that trip. So why not drive through Kansas, Nebraska, Iowa, and Wisconsin and sneak up on Chicago from the north? Yes, it will be a longer, more expensive drive but you'll get there eventually. What you've done is to approach your goal from a different direction than the direct path and you've taken more time to reach that goal allowing your inner self to adjust to the once uncomfortable goal. That's how you set and achieve a goal that is outside of your comfort zone.

You've looked at your inner desires and what makes you feel all happy inside. From there you've figured out some shorter-term goals that you want to achieve. Myself, I'd like to lose thirty pounds however I really do enjoy eating all those bad things. So I've got some internal conflicts to iron out and I will, eventually. You have figured out by now that you like associating with people, working with numbers, playing with the computer, enjoy physical exertion, etc. It's time to review what job you currently have and see how many of those inner desires and capabilities you are fulfilling. List out those current job assignments that don't seem to fit, and list out other assignments that you think would be a good fit for you. So now you have a beginning state and a future state. You are good at handling people on the phone but you'd really rather be dealing with people face-to-face. Hmmm, sounds like a goal in the making. Or, you deal with data all day long and would rather be out there discovering the data instead. Maybe another goal waiting to be defined?

You get the drift don't you? I am not going to give you a goal in life, neither is your mother or your current boss. It all has to come from within you and others can only suggest possible goals for you depending on their limited knowledge of who you are inside.

Ok now it's time for the next step, planning to achieve your goals. Like any road trip, how you get to your destination is at least as important as the destination. Your path can be long and tortuous with lots of back-tracking and unexpected detours, or your path can be fairly direct and cut and dried. You may like the experiences of the unknown and therefore take the long way around, or you may like the tried and true straight-line drive because it's the destination that counts; that is purely your choice based on what you feel inside. I'm pretty much a no-nonsense person so I tend to go with the more direct routes yet I know others that prefer the lure of the unknown so they just go wherever the wind blows them. *There is no one correct plan to achieve a goal; there is only the path that works for you.*

When I go to the grocery store, I take the shortest quickest route because the goal of reaching the grocery store is a very minor goal in my mind so I don't want to put much planning into it. However, when we took a driving vacation to see Yellowstone National Park and Mt. Rushmore, I also included quite a few side trips and allowed for plenty of time to do detours as they might come up. That trip was a much more major goal and I allowed for those last-minute changes to the itinerary. We could have made it back from Mt. Rushmore to our home in about three ten-hour driving days but we spent five days to allow for some pit stops to see other things that came up along the route. The goal was not to make it there and back in as short of time as possible, but to use whatever time to see what else was out there. You've probably been on a guided tour of something at some time and I bet dollars to doughnuts that at some point on that tour you wanted to look over something a bit more but the guide was already shooing you on to the next stopping point. If it is a simple or minor goal, the plan to get there doesn't have to be complicated. But if the goal is not only to get someplace but also to enjoy the journey, you want to spend more time in developing the plan. So the point of this is that *the importance of the goal determines the complexity of the plan to get there.*

How do you plan to achieve your goals? The simplest way to start is to list out the basic requirements. On that drive to Yellowstone, the very basic requirement was determining how many days we were going to be gone. That required knowing how many miles it was from our house to Yellowstone along with the speed limits on the preferred highways which gave us how many hours it would take to drive there and back. Dividing this by the hours per day we were willing to drive gave us the approximate number of days we would be on the road (or you could do the easy thing and use various internet map programs). From that point we looked at cities to stop in for the night that matched the approximate miles we'd be driving per day. You can see where this is going. By starting with very basic requirements we were able to come up with an outline for our trip with plenty of time for sight-seeing if the opportunities arose. Another key part of our plan was some research on just what sights to see while we were in the neighborhood. From this some side trips got planned and the overall itinerary got some minor revisions. Without the research, I would have never known that Devil's Tower in Wyoming was just a 90-mile detour from our planned route, and I would never have gotten those scenic photos to commemorate our trip and the bragging rights about "I've been there".

So you want to be that airline pilot. Let's start with making a plan to get there. There is plenty of information out there on the qualifications of airline pilots as well as many different flying schools for gaining a private pilot's license, so it shouldn't be that difficult starting a list of the necessary qualifications. This is where you'll have to do some basic research; remember that nothing comes without some effort on your part. Gather the information and now it is time to figure out where you stand in meeting those qualifications. Find where you are lacking the necessary skills or education, and go do some more research on how you can gain those skills and education. You may find that if you take certain classes at the nearby community college you can meet most of the educational requirements and then if you take classes at the private pilot school at the airport thirty miles north, you will meet the very basic requirements to be considered a candidate at the local airline. You have just assembled the basic plan for achieving your goal. There will be other details to fill in such as how much this is going to cost in time and dollars, when those classes are offered at the college, how long this is going to take overall, and when you might be able to finally apply for and be hired as an airline pilot.

Now comes the difficult part, assessing your plan and goal. You look at your plan and it turns out that you will have to take six classes in addition to pilot school but those classes are only offered sequentially so it's going to take the better part of two years to get through those classes. It's also going to cost you a total of nine thousand dollars to take all those classes and flight school. Now is the time to decide whether or not that airline pilot goal is worth the time and money that you're going to invest just to get to the point of being employable – remember you won't automatically be an airline pilot when you complete all the requirements. So is the goal worth it or not? That is up to you only. If you want to go through with it, you've already got the basics of the plan to achieve that goal. If you decide not to go through with it, start exploring parallel jobs such as flight attendant, air traffic controller, etc. along with going back to examining how that original airline pilot goal fit in with your inner desires and drives. If you wanted to be an airline pilot but you wanted to be able to apply next week for that job, you've just discovered through your research how unrealistic your original goal was. If you can reconcile that goal with the proposed plan, i.e. get over wanting to achieve it 'now', then go with it. If you're not willing to spend the time and money involved, time for a new goal.

So in the simplest form, making a plan to achieve a goal starts with the basic requirements. Main questions to answer are what skills and knowledge do I have now, and what are the new skills and requirements that I require to reach my goal? From there you have to figure out the gaps and how you can acquire those missing skills and knowledge. That is your basic plan to achieve your goal.

Let's take the simplest goal that almost all employees have – how do I get a promotion and bigger paycheck? Most big companies and all unionized companies have lists of the job requirements for the various levels of employees. If these do not exist for your company or job assignment, ask around and especially ask your boss "what does it take for me to get a promotion?" then make a list. From these lists, you can easily tell where you are now and what is needed to get to the next level. List out what skills you need or what knowledge you need to demonstrate, and then look for a way to get those missing pieces. Sometimes you can take classes inside or outside the company while other situations might require just more time in the job. This can be the building blocks of your basic plan for getting the promotion. Warning, this plan of yours is not going to be a slam dunk for you getting the promotion, there are still going to be outside influences on your plan so do not be thinking that if you plan it, it will happen – that was the major flaw in that seminar that I mentioned earlier. I've worked with a lot of people over the years and one thing always stands out with working with the newer employees. I've been asked many many times "how do I get an upgrade?". One person I was mentoring not long ago even went as far as to ask me "how do I convince my boss that I'm awesome and deserve an upgrade?". Questions like that usually irritate me to some extent because all the information is right there if the people just looked for it. Also, I consider 'being awesome' an earned response rather than an inborn genetic attribute. Again, your career is up to you and if you don't want to put the effort into making it a successful career, that's really too bad.

Last note: don't go overboard with publicizing your personal goals and how you have plans to achieve this or that. People will not react well to what they will perceive as a single-mindedness to achieve that goal. Some of that will be envy that you have goals and some of that will be perceived as egotistical behavior on your part. I had one manager that broadcast loud and clear that his goal was to become a vice-president. He had that goal and boy did he have a plan to get there. He had mapped out his career at least 10 years into the future. He 'knew' that in 3 years' time he would transfer to this job assignment, then spend a couple years there, then transfer to the next job assignment, etc. with specifics and dates and all the rest of the gory details. My problem with him was that he made it mandatory that everyone working for him also make their own plans for the next at least half-dozen years. I'm sorry but I don't have a crystal ball that will tell me exactly what the next year will bring let alone multiple years. Besides, if working for him for another two or three years was the immediate future, my plan would consist of just how I was going to get out from under his control. I remember in a couple meetings where he was explaining his plan, I asked a couple non-confrontational questions about how we were supposed to set our plans up and what goals should we be using. He went into how one of our immediate goals was to take all the training that was recommended. When I asked where the list of classes was written down so that we could compare that with what we had already taken, he got actually kind of snotty and told me/us "if you don't know what training you need then you don't need to be working for me". I think half the group breathed a sigh of relief at that because none of us knew where this magical list of classes was and were looking for any excuse to get out from under this guy. It was maybe a week or two later that this manager went to see the guy that I was reporting to for daily assignments and told him I was abrasive, stubborn, and not a team player so he was considering transferring me out and did the other manager mind? My manager told him I was doing quite well and that he didn't see any of those qualities in me so he wanted me to stay. That was the beginning of 'Mr. Goals' campaign to really smear me and poison people against me that lasted for the better part of 9 months (I heard about most of it through a higher-level manager that happened to be a good friend). And the outcome of this was ironic because people began to take notice more and more of how obnoxious Mr. Goals actually was and it culminated in his boss transferring him to a subsidiary location and effectively burying him in podunksville. I didn't have anything to do with all this, I believe he just lost his cool when I started asking questions and people saw that he was being vindictive to a valued employee, namely me.

Summary point:

Review your inner desires, needs, wants, and aptitudes before setting a goal that meshes so that you will experience the most success when you ultimately achieve your goal. Do not lock yourself into a few long-term goals but allow yourself the flexibility to make mid-course corrections including revising your goals or setting new goals. To achieve your goals, do your homework and find out what it takes to get to your goal from where you are now and evaluate whether or not reaching that goal is worth the effort you must put into it. If it is, then use your homework to assemble your basic plan to achieve your goal. If your goal is deemed unrealistic or not worth the effort you're going to have to put into it, go back to reviewing your desires and wants and see if there are different goals that will fill the bill. And lastly and perhaps most importantly, *your goals and plans to achieve them are only going to be as good as the effort you put into them.*

Understanding and working with various personalities

Now we finally get to the fun part of working for a living and that is dealing with those other people you get to work with. Up to now, I've been speaking mainly about looking inside yourself to figure out what you want to do in life and how you can get there from here. It's time to figure out how to actually work with other people.

Everyone has their own base personality and most show more than one personality depending on circumstances. Think of it this way; when you are at the grocery store looking for something specific you are usually going to act more forcefully with the store clerk than if you were asking for something that your partner had put in the pantry (maybe not?). An important key to being a success at work is to figure out your co-workers' usual personalities so that you can establish a good working relationship with them. Once you do that, you will find that work will go easier and smoother. If you've ever been in a workplace where people got on each other's nerves all the time, it probably wasn't a pleasant place to work and not a very productive place either. If you can work with the other people, you'll find that the workplace functions better and it's easier on your stress level.

Stress is an important piece of this workplace puzzle with personalities. If you find that your job or workplace is stressful, it's going to show in your performance and in your health sooner or later. I have to take prescription antacids for the rest of my life because once I got a new boss that wasn't familiar with the job at all and rode the people as if it were an army camp. I considered getting the job done as number one priority so I spent quite some effort in keeping the rest of the group from open mutiny. After about two years of that the boss got rotated into another assignment but I was left with a bad case of acid reflux that burned away a portion of my esophagus. The messages from this are: stress is self-imposed, and stress is guaranteed to take its toll sooner or later.

There are many classes and books out there that will help you cope with stress and I've taken a couple of those classes. I'm not an expert but one thing that showed up in every class was how you can lower your stress level by identifying other people's personalities and then modifying your interaction with them to *keep the interaction productive instead of contentious*. Therefore, let's explore some of the different stereotypical personalities you'll find yourself working with sooner or later.

"The Lord of the Manor" is that person that's usually pretty easy to get along with until they need to get something done. Then they casually drop by your desk and ask "oh I have this little thing to do and I'm tied up with this other thing, so would you mind taking care of it for me?". Yes, they're the person that believes some of their job assignments are just beneath their level and they're always dropping some of them off on other people's desks. I'm *not* talking about the co-worker that comes by in desperation and says "I've been working on this but the boss wants me to get this other thing done RIGHT NOW so could you please take care of this other thing for me?". So how do you deal with The Lord of the Manor? If you accept the job you will have to keep accepting those jobs because The Lord of the Manor will see you as a sucker and keep dumping stuff on you. There are a couple ways you can deal with this person besides just accepting their work. You can look them coldly in the eye and say "do your own g-damn work" which will gain you an office enemy; you can say "I'll do it this one time since I'm not that busy" which leaves you open for a recurrence any time you don't look super busy; or you can say "I don't have time either but let me show you how I would complete this" which brings the situation back to focusing on the job at hand. In the first two responses, you are bringing perceptions and personalities into the picture while the last response pertains to only the job. That is what you must do, bring it back to the job and *leave the personality out of it*. If you offer to show them how to do it, you are letting them know that you are not going to do their job for them. If they agree, then that actually puts you in a better spot because now you are the authority figure teaching them how to do it. If they don't agree, they probably won't be coming back again asking you to do their job, so you win in either case.

"Dr. Doom" is an interesting person because all they know is that whatever they do and no matter how hard they try; things are going to fail. Whether they actually do or not is questionable because if they truly failed at everything, they most likely wouldn't be employed for too long. They also believe that any new process or procedure isn't going to work so why even try to improve the processes. Dealing with this personality isn't easy because they are so negative. I remember presenting a plan for borrowing components from several products in work to be able to assemble a single product for testing purposes. Before I got through the overall concept of the plan Dr. Doom jumped into the conversation with "that's the absolute stupidest thing I've ever heard, you don't know sh-t, you couldn't make a plan to get to the bathroom" and so forth. I hadn't expected the ferocity of the attack but instead of feeding Dr. Doom with more material and escalating the conflict with a few choice swear words, I stayed calm and repeatedly asked what the major flaws in my concept were. Once the director saw that I was trying to have a constructive conversation he intervened and told Dr. Doom to "shut up and just let him get through the plan before you sh-t all over him again". Dr. Doom left the conference room in a huff and I proceeded to run through the rest of my plan, which the director praised as pretty damn smart and really looked like the best way to go. The key to working with a Dr. Doom is to not allow them to continue saying the sky is falling but to cut them off after each and every point they try to make and ask, in a non-confrontational way, "what do you think causes that?" and "how do you think we can get around that?". In this way, you are engaging with their thinking mind instead of their reactive mind. If you deny them the opportunity to vent at least a little, or if you allow them to vent exceedingly, all that's going to happen is their reactive mind is going to blow and you'll get the full force of their displeasure. *Always bring the focus back to the situation at hand and ignore the personality.*

Some doom-and-gloomers aren't combative at all; they just sit there and let the world go by. Those people you have to try and get involved again and the only way to do it is the same as I've outlined above, when they start forecasting that the sky is about to fall, break in on their litany and ask what they think should be done. In the best instances, you will probably see them get a puzzled look on their face as they actually try to think about the fact that someone asked for their idea (not opinion). In the worst case, you'll get a "I don't know" and then silence. Engage their thinking mind instead of their reactionary mind and you may find them quite a bit easier to deal with. But for god's sake, don't yell at them because you'll never hear another thing from them ever again.

"The General" can be a difficult person to work with at first, especially since The General believes everyone else works for them. This is the person that is always ordering other people around, sometimes forcefully, and sometimes in a softer manner by saying things like "what you should have done was …". The know how to solve just about everything but people don't pay attention to them so that's why things are always broken, at least that's the way The General's mind works. The General can be an asset though, if you know how to use them. The General needs to take charge of projects because they know 'the best way', so keep asking questions of them such as "what would you do?" and keep them reacting to you instead of letting them be in the driver's seat. In this way you are also giving The General an active role in determining the plan. Once you get the basics of your project plan together, then is the time that you put The General on stage with the presentation and implementation of the plan. Their natural 'take charge' attitude can be used to push plan approvals through and also to oversee the implementation. Once you get The General reacting to you (you can 'steer' them with a little bit of effort) instead of going off half-cocked at everyone in sight, you'll find that working with them isn't so bad after all.

"the mouse" is that person that gets selected to be on one of those infamous cross-functional teams and spends their entire time sitting in the corner and not saying a word. They come to meetings, they agree with just about everything said, and have no ideas or opinions of their own. In this way they are similar to Dr. Doom because they just don't think any of their ideas are worth it. There are ways to draw them out of their shell but it's going to be a bit painful. One thing that always helps is to repeatedly ask for their ideas and if they don't express any, start floating ideas past them and repeatedly asking for their opinion. It's usually best to handle this on a one-on-one situation since they will be afraid of their own shadow in open meetings. The key to working with this type of person is patience, lots and lots of patience. Don't ask the mouse to lead a team because they won't be able to do it. They are good at working on a specific task or working as the go-fer for the next personality. And watch out for a mouse being overly emotional; sometimes they perceive they are getting yelled at when all you've done is make critical comments that may be too strong for their personality. I remember telling one person that they were going down an iffy path with solving a problem and it would be easier if they did plan B.

The person actually ran to the bathroom to cry for about 10 minutes. I didn't know that there was a problem until someone else came by and said that other person was crying because I yelled at them. I swear I didn't yell but the other person took it that way so I had to wait for a bit and then go apologize for what they felt. So it's not only what you think, it's how the other person receives also.

"The Used Car Salesman" is that person that is the stereotype of those people you see on television. They are loud, quick to take action, can't wait for decisions to be made so that action can be taken, and generally have limited attention spans. They get impatient with problem solving processes and frequently only pay lip-service to those processes. That's the down side of Used Car Salesmen but that can also be used to your advantage. Because of their impatience, they can be used to push others to get work done. They can also be phenomenal pitch-men for pushing a new product or process through. So use them to provide the incentive to get things done. Don't put the Used Car Salesman in a position doing research because they won't have the patience for it and the research results will be spotty at best. The Used Car Salesman is good at making decisions based on limited data so use them in that manner. There have been plenty of teams I've been on where we literally spent months gathering data and endlessly discussing in exquisitely painful detail all the data we gathered. I didn't see it then but what we needed was a Used Car Salesman to make the decision and push it through.

Just the opposite, "Sheep" are competent and easy people to work with but they won't make a decision. They are the ones who are always asking "what do you want me to do now?". Given a specific assignment they are quite good at getting it done, but they won't go out of their way to find problems in the making. "This doesn't seem right, or like it will work, what should I do?" is their way of solving problems that are fermenting and waiting to explode. There are two main reasons for them acting the way they do; lack of self-confidence, or being used to working under "The General" and being ordered around every day. They need to be led or at least pointed in the right direction most of the time. An easy way to deal with them is when they ask "what should I do?" to answer with "what do you think might work?". With this response you are giving them the green light to act because most of the time, they know perfectly well what is at least the immediate first step to take. They need a boost of self-confidence that their inclinations are most likely the way to solve the situation and that's what you try to give them by asking for their opinion. However, some of them might also have a chip on their shoulder in regards to management. I have heard people many times make the comment "if only management would let us …". Let me say this about that comment: If the results of a project are forecasted as positive, there aren't many managers around that will say "absolutely not". Sheep are also the ones who ask for 'empowerment' from management. Heck, most managers don't care how you do your job, just so long as it gets done satisfactorily, on-time, and on-budget, so the ones asking to be empowered are those people afraid to take the responsibility for their actions. The contention by those Sheep is if management hasn't empowered them, then its management's responsibility if something goes wrong. And that's a total cop-out. All employees are empowered to do the right thing but maybe some of them wanted to do something earlier and were told no by their manager. So now they are going to pout and only do what their manager 'commands' them to do and if it screws up, well then it's the manager's fault not theirs. Just about the only way around this empowerment barrier is to announce that you are taking the responsibility which will let them off the hook. Trying to push them to accept responsibility is usually a lost cause because like real four-legged sheep, once they get something in their head it will take a really big hammer to knock it out of there.

'The Jokester" on the other hand is not paying attention to a whole lot of anything in the workplace. They liven up the workplace for sure but they don't get a whole lot done. It may look like they're getting work done but in most cases, someone else (usually 'the mouse') is picking up the slack for them. These people need to be reminded that they have work to do and that sometimes one has to get serious in order to get the job done correctly. They sit around and talk for most of the day, usually recounting funny stories or humorous events that have happened to them, their family, or to people on the internet. Some amount of that is great for morale because it reminds everyone that there is a life outside work, but too much can bog down the rest of the team. It isn't easy getting 'The Jokester" to settle down and get some work done and sometimes it takes measures as drastic as setting quotas for output in order for them to see that work is indeed a place where people are expected to work. Otherwise, an occasional "hey I got to get this out real quick" comment or the tried and true method of simply turning your back and picking up your own assignment will work. When the audience is gone, "The Jokester" will usually settle down for a bit and focus more on their work.

"The Wizard" is a great person to know because they've usually been around a long time and know just about all the ins and outs of the job. They may claim they don't know everything and that every day they learn something new, but they're the ones who really know how everything works. They're usually fairly quiet about doing their work but as you watch over time, you'll see that they get a lot of people dropping by to ask questions of them. They don't go out of their way to teach anyone or share their knowledge, only when asked a direct question will they explain how everything works together. They are the backbone of the workplace because they've been there long enough to see the majority of situations that tend to arise from time to time. But the problem is they don't actively train anyone. So this is the person you drop by to chat with and then coax them to impart their knowledge with questions about "how does this work?" or "how do you get from here to there?". I once worked with a Wizard a long time ago. By the time I met him he had already been working there for more than twenty years. He knew all kinds of trivia and little tidbits about odd procedures but he just wasn't spreading any of that knowledge around. My boss had to openly tell him that he needed to train me before he started opening that chamber of secret knowledge that he had. He was a great guy but until he was ordered, he wasn't letting go of anything. These are the only two ways I know of to get this person to share; by you continuing to ask questions and by having their boss order it. They usually do a brilliant job on their own but if they leave, a big hole in the competency of the group opens up.

"The Yeller" is an easy person to understand. They yell when things go wrong, they yell when someone asks a question, they yell when they drop a hammer, and they yell when they miss the garbage can with their used paper towels. They yell, often using very colorful and sometimes embarrassing language, at just about everything. That's because under that gruff exterior is someone who is not happy doing what they're doing, so they allow their anger to come out. It isn't necessarily your fault something happened but they'll yell at you none-the-less. How do you deal with someone who's so angry all the time? I've tried humor and gotten occasional positive results but not enough to warrant putting that as a solution. Something that works a little better is to sound like you're agreeing with them but you have to say it right so you're actually being neutral. Let's try a couple possibilities and start with the yeller saying "What idiot put this garbage can right next to the door to the men's room?". You could try to make light of the matter by asking "what's the matter, stub your toe?" but that will probably provoke them to respond "g-damn right, what f-ing moron thought that this was where it should go?" and you haven't really calmed them down at all. On the other hand, if you tried "you're right that those garbage cans can be dangerous, where should it really go?" you're more likely to get a lower key response back from them. You're focusing on the situation, not any of the people or personalities involved and this shorts out the yeller's reactive mind and starts their thinking mind because you've asked them a question that requires active thought on their part.

The last main stereotypical personality I'll mention is "The Rulebook". Just like it says, this person likes to follow the rules and if the ship sinks under them as they are following the rules, so be it. This person is so black and white about everything that they usually end up infuriating everyone around them. If the rules say that you have to have this form filled out in this way, by hell they are going to make sure that form is filled out – make no mistake about it, they normally don't do a whole lot themselves but rather look over other people's shoulders and tell them that the rules say the job has to be done this way, not the way that the other person is doing it. One of the big reasons for quoting the rules so often and trying to make sure that everyone follows them is because inside they are fairly insecure in their own capabilities and thought processes. They are also prone to being perfectionists in all that they do which in itself is not a bad thing to be because it shows that they will do their due diligence on any job that they actually do accomplish. But they are afraid of making a decision or going outside the rules because if they fail or something goes wrong they will be blamed and they can't tolerate failure. They want something to fall back on, e.g., "the rules" so they can blame the rules for producing an erroneous outcome and not take the blame themselves. So what can you do with this personality? How can you work with them and more importantly how can you get them to be a contributing source to the general workplace instead of being everyone's pain in the backside? There are a couple ways to utilize them and the first is to find that job assignment where there is literally no leeway in the rules, i.e., as the quality control person in charge of making sure that the burger is cooked at 350 degrees for no less than 7 minutes, or the person who makes sure that when this product goes out the door it has all the necessary routing slips and documentation with it, or the person in charge of shipping who makes sure that every order is filled correctly and sent to the correct buyer. That's the best solution but since those types of job assignments may not be available, what if that person is part of your team tasked with solving a problem? Most problem-solving teams start with a review of the current situation and that's where The Rulebook comes in handy because they can be assigned to research what is happening and what are the procedures governing the process. But what if you're not on a team with this person, you're just sitting next to them in your office so what do you do with them now? Give them the assignment to do the documentation of how you are supposed to do your job. They actually love going through procedures and directives and compiling the process "as it should be". Then building off what they have compiled, you can start asking intelligent questions such as "why does step 4 say to do this when step 9 says not to do this?" and then start them on working on a new or revised set of procedures. Recognize what they are good at and use it, don't get angry and tell them "oh go blow your rules out your butt-hole" because that will just antagonize them and give them more reason to prove that what they read in the rules is the only way to do the job.

Over the years, I've had people call me down to the shop floor and then proceed to swear for a couple minutes straight about how this isn't working worth two sh-ts, whoever dreamed this up is a complete f-ing moron, etc. My response usually was to let them blow off some steam and then come right back with "what do you suggest?" and go from there. I found that this was the easiest way to deal with them because I was allowing them the chance to express their opinion, thereby acknowledging that I gave some respect to them as a person, and then asking what they thought of as a solution which further acknowledged that I thought they were of value. Treat people with respect and most of the time you'll get paid back in the same manner.

If you understand the personality that is being shown to you when you interact with another person, you can tailor your responses and interaction to either cut off negative behavior or encourage positive behavior. In almost all cases, if you focus on the situation or problem at hand and ignore any of the people or personalities involved, you will show the person you're interacting with your cool calm personality, one that gets problems and situations solved before they explode into major catastrophes. One infamous time I used this was when I had to discipline one of my workers for mooning a secretary (yes this really happened). He claimed he unbuckled his belt to adjust his pants and his pants slid down a bit in the process. She claimed it was a full moon that happened. Since nobody else could confirm either side of the story I was forced into an oral warning with him. I focused solely on the situation, namely that "adjusting one's pants" was something that should only occur in the men's room and not in the office proper, to which he agreed. If I had gone into "that was really a stupid thing to do" I would have given him the opportunity to respond in kind, most likely to the detriment of the secretary, and also would have given him the idea that I thought he was stupid. Keeping to the facts in the matter kept it lower-key and allowed the two of us to reach an agreement that this was definitely not going to happen again.

It does no good and is actually counter-productive to yell back at the yeller, or to tell the general to put it where the sun don't shine. All you're doing with those people is upping the ante in terms of how much of their temper they are going to let go. If the yeller says "what moron came up with this?" and you respond with "a smarter moron than you" you're not going to get much further in that conversation before getting something thrown at you. If the general tells you "you should have done it this way instead" and you respond "who the f- do you think you are, Albert Einstein?", or as one of my bosses used to say "who died and made you God?", that conversation is going down the toilet pretty quickly. So stick with the facts of the situation and leave the personalities out of it, you'll be more successful and more importantly you'll probably live longer.

By the way, over the years I've been called all sorts of names with some of them being quite colorful (one of the more intriguing was "mother f-ing son of a g-damn whoring sh-t eating b-tch"), and I never let any of them get to me or affect the way I do my work. It's just a word or phrase meant to bring me down to the speaker's level, nothing more. My thought was if they don't respect me yet, they soon will due to my work performance.

As an added bonus, let me say a few words about Personnel, Human Resources, or whatever the organization dealing with people issues is called in your company. Yes, you can go to them and find out all about what the genuine workplace rules are; those things that are hard and fast such as what you can be fired for. You can lodge complaints with them if you are the victim of a crime but do not think that they are there for you. Burn this into your mind – *they are there to protect the company.* Part of that responsibility is to make sure that the workplace rules are enforced without regard to race, creed, or color but that does not mean that they are there to protect you from what you may think is 'bad treatment' from your boss or coworkers. If your boss is indeed mistreating you, HR will usually take some action but only from the viewpoint of protecting the company from possible litigation and not to protect you as a worker. I had a manager once that decided that he didn't want me in his group anymore so he snooped around until he found an opening in another department, made an appointment for me with the hiring manager, and then out of the blue presented me on a Tuesday morning with a "I made an appointment for you to go work for x and you have until Friday to pack up your desk". I went to see HR and they had a little chat with him about violating the workplace transfer rules, but other than that, HR basically told me "you'd better find a new job". So do not rely on HR to protect you because that is not their job.

Summary point:

Learn to pick up signals from the people you're dealing with, identify the main personality that you're dealing with, and react accordingly. Keep your focus on the assignment and keep your temper in check or you won't have a successful experience. I'm not saying play suck-up to people you have to work with because that will just mark you with a target on your forehead that says "kick me". *Keep the interaction to business but tailor your comments and questions to the personality you're dealing with and you will be successful eventually.*

Solving problems by first finding them

Why would you want to go looking for problems when there's a stack of them on your desk already? Because solving problems that haven't yet come to fruition means that the task will be easier because you won't have to clean up the mess once the problem comes to a head. If there is a bucket of mop water in the middle of the kitchen floor and there's a bunch of people constantly moving through the kitchen, sooner or later someone is going to kick that bucket over and dirty water is going to go everywhere. Why not before that happens pick up the bucket and put it next to the slop sink or better yet empty it? It's a whole lot easier to spend the 30 seconds now to avoid spending the 15 minutes later mopping up that water when it spills all over. In the same vein, keeping an eye out for potential problems and making mid-course corrections to the plan of action can keep at least some of those "oh crap, really screwed the pooch this time" situations from happening. *If you can spend ten minutes now reviewing the plan while it is in work, you could save hours later that would have been spent going back over the plan to see where it started to fall apart.*

So how can you foretell when there's going to be a problem? Unless you have a magic time machine that allows you to see tomorrow or a week into the future, you can't. The best you're going to be able to do is to predict the possibility of something going wrong and take action from there. If it's a low probability of occurring or a low or insignificant outcome, then the need to take action beforehand is also lessened (not eliminated). If there is a high probability of occurring or a major consequence, then it behooves you to take some action now to lessen the chance and the consequence. And how do you determine which it's going to be? By researching and looking in depth at the process as it should be and how it is planned to be. Now look at the capabilities of the people performing the job and match those with the requirements of the job. For example, if you have people assigned to do the job that are relative newcomers the chance of something going sideways is correspondingly higher than if you have an experienced crew. The same for a complicated process, the more steps there are the higher the chance of something going wrong. If you are breaking in a brand new person as a short-order chef with instructions that their job is to season the uncooked hamburger patty, then lightly oil the grill after making sure it is heated to at least 400 degrees, fry the patty for 3 minutes on the first side then an additional 4 minutes after flipping it over, lightly butter the bottom piece of the bun, then place on the grill for the last minute the burger is cooking to brown it lightly, smear two tablespoons of secret sauce on the upper half of the bun and set aside, in addition make sure that there is one half-cup of shredded lettuce plus two slices of tomato to put on the hamburger, then assemble in order of lower bun, lettuce, hamburger, tomato, and top bun half. For a new cook this will take them a lot of time to put out the first dozen or so hamburgers and they will get some of them wrong. So there's a problem in the making here. One way to get around this is to do at least one demonstration for them and then give them a pictorial sheet that shows what goes where and when. This visual reminder will allow your new employee to use their own abilities to match what the picture says should be the final product. There are other ways to help them out such as to lay out the ingredients in sequence order, so you should explore many different ideas. Some things are as easy as "wash potato, dry with a paper towel, then put in the oven at 350 degrees for 90 minutes" to make a baked potato, while others such as making a wild rice stuffed flank steak take a little more instruction and attention to detail.

Give people a chance to succeed and you'll find that they actually do more often than not.

In one of my last job assignments, I wrote the instructions for how to assemble various components into a completed assembly. This involved using rivets, screws, and adhesives. I had to take into account that some of the people doing those jobs had a lot of experience while others had very little experience. I had to walk a fine line with my instructions by being specific enough that the novices could understand the steps yet not offend the experienced people by saying things like "using a #10 flat head screwdriver, tighten the screws". You've all had the same experience with those toys or barbecues where "some assembly is required". The steps to follow need to be clear enough that anyone of any experience level could follow them. And this is the first step in short-circuiting potential problems. Make the process steps clear enough that anyone can follow.

But sooner or later, a problem is going to come up. How do you solve it? In some cases, the errant step is going to be very evident but in others the real problem is going to be hiding behind a lot of static. Look at it this way, when you go to your doctor with the complaint that "my right side hurts", the doctor is going to go through a series of steps to diagnose just what the cause is before prescribing any treatment. Your right side could be hurting because of a muscle strain, or something you ate, or various other things including gall bladder problems or appendicitis. The doctor asks clarifying questions to rule out the chaff and then makes an educated guess as to what the true cause is. You are going to have to do the same with problems that occur.

And this should not be new to you, in fact you already do this unconsciously all day long. "My pen isn't working right" and then you take off the cap or click it to make sure that the writing nib is exposed, if so then you drag the nib on a piece of scrap paper and see if there is just a glob of dried ink on the nib, if not then you observe if any ink is deposited on the paper, if not then check whether there is any ink left in the reservoir, if not then the pen is dead and a new one is needed. Your shoe is sliding around on your foot when you walk around so you check to see if your laces are untied and if they are then you tie them, if not then you untie and retie them tighter to see if that works. So you do this step by step problem solving process every day and that is what you need to do with problems that surface in the workplace.

Start by listing out what the problem is, then list out the various things that might cause the problem. Ask yourself at each step "why did this happen or what causes this?" then list the various possible causes. Continue asking why those possible causes may have happened and expanding your tree. Sooner or later (some call this "the five why's" because usually five levels are sufficient to get to the root cause), you will get to that root cause or causes of what is really the problem. I had a 35mm camera one time that worked just great, until we took a trip to Florida. I took lots of photos while we were there but when the film was developed almost every picture had a dark blurry edge that gradually increased until the last roll of film was hardly more than complete dark blurs. I thought about the various causes, the film was bad, the film wasn't processed correctly, the camera lens was dirty, something else was wrong with the camera, etc. I went down through each of these possible causes and investigated to find the real cause. It turned out that because we stayed in an air conditioned hotel for part of the day and then spent hours walking around in Florida's hot humid climate the rest of the day, condensation formed on the inside of the camera lens and this led to actual mold growth on the inside of the camera, hence the progressively darker and darker photos. The camera was a total write-off since nobody could assure me that they'd be able to clean all of the mold out and there was a very good chance that it would just grow back again.

So when you find a problem that has occurred, ask why it could have happened. Take those possible causes and again ask why they might have occurred. Was the problem because the person involved didn't have the necessary skills, then was that caused by a lack of training or incorrect training?

Here's where all that data that gets collected and stored in today's computer age comes in handy. Since just about everything connected with orders these days is generated or stored via computers, there is a wealth of data out there that can be mined. And don't just confine yourself to one area or type of data, see what can be found out by combining or correlating different sets of data. One example I can give you is when I queried the quality database and correlated it with the customer order database. I was able to point out that certain customers ordered unique items and those unique items accounted for a significant number of errors in our manufacturing shops. From this I was able to put together a set of familiarization 'classes' that I taught to the shop people in advance of those customers' orders hitting the shops. I was also able to get the shop schedulers to schedule extra time for those orders. The result was a significant reduction in shop errors. Another example was that the shop people were having problems locating components in their correct position on assemblies since the components were used multiple times per assembly and not always in the same place. I got one of our programmers to combine information from two different databases, use that information to query a third database, and then produce a 'map' for each of the more than one hundred assemblies showing the exact location of each component that would print out whenever that assembly was ordered.

A couple final words on problem solving. For any problem, a possible solution that must be considered is "do nothing" or do nothing permanent. Some problems occur as just plain flukes, statistically improbable occurrences that really should never happen but due to a fantastic

47

convergence of variables did happen. Or, here's a problem and the only solution that will make sure it never happens again is going to cost so much that it just isn't worth it. In this case, you may want to incorporate other palliative adjustments that may lessen the impact or lessen the incidence. But never ignore the possibility that doing nothing may be the best solution. The product with the problems may be phased out within a certain time period meaning that it just isn't worth it to solve the problem but merely to band-aid it until product obsolescence may be the best answer.

Some more last words on problem solving that sometimes baffles people is "if you automate a process that has errors, all you've done is automate the generation of those errors". Take the situation where someone with a problem says "we've got lots of problems with hand-assembling this so we'll just bring in a robot to assemble it". Chances are really good that if you do this, that robot is going to turn out less good product than hand-assembling ever did. The problem is not the hand-assembling, it's something else, either in the design or in the assembly steps that is causing the problems. If you merely automate the process of assembling those parts, you've just guaranteed bad products as a result. Humans are quite adaptable and ingenious in figuring out things and working around others while machines do exactly what they are programmed to do. There's the story of the shop that was assembling fishing pole segments together but had a rather high scrap rate. One solution considered was automation to remove the human element. But after some research, one older worker was found to be consistently the top performer in terms of quality output even though they weren't the fastest person in the shop. Someone actually took a look at her step by step process and found that at a certain step the worker was rubbing their finger on their face, then spreading the resultant facial oil on the mating ends of the fishing rods to make them go together more easily. The other workers would just force the ends together which every now and then resulted in split ends which were only good for the garbage can. If the existing process had been automated, the assembly machine would have had the same problems as the other workers and there would have been more split ends. By finding out that just that little bit of lubricant made the rod ends go together without splitting, the whole shop was able to dramatically reduce their scrap rates thus making automation of the process not economically sound.

Summary point:

In any work environment, and especially in your plans to reach your goals, there are opportunities for things to go wrong or produce undesirable results. Finding these speed-bumps and figuring out ways to make them easier, simpler, and more fool-proof will increase the probability of success in the long run. When problems do occur, starting with what happened and working your way back through the various levels of "why it happened" will eventually lead to the root cause or causes of the problem which will then allow plans to be made and implemented to ensure that the problems are reduced or eliminated. In all cases, the feasibility of the corrective action must be reviewed to ensure that it is economically sound. This is an important point when considering automation as the corrective action.

Reporting successes and making the presentation that impresses everyone

Your boss comes to you Wednesday morning and says "the director has you on the agenda for 20 minutes at the staff meeting next Monday afternoon to explain what you did with that hot job last week".

What are you going to do? Start squealing "no no no, this can't happen to me", or snorting "what the heck are they poking their noses into my job for?", or grunting "uhhh yeah sure". Yes, you have to prepare a presentation or report on something you did, so really, what are you going to do?

First of all, this is not the end of the world (unless you completely botch it), rather it could be the beginning of a whole new world with greater responsibility and freedom of action if you handle it correctly.

The first thing to do is ask your boss for more clarification on just what is expected. Your boss probably has a fairly good idea of what is being looked for so use that source to at least start an outline of the salient points that need covering in your presentation. Your boss may even give you an outline of what should be presented.

Once you have some idea of what you have to put together, start breaking down the task into the three most important segments: Content, Format, and Presentation. Content is just what you are going to talk about. You should, with your boss's agreement, put boundaries on what you are going to show. You don't want to start with the first chapter of Genesis and go through the whole Old Testament when all you really want to talk about is the walls of Jericho coming down. You also have to figure out just what the point is going to be, is it the solution or the situation that led up to it. Format is how you are going to physically present your story. Do you need charts, graphs, pictures, or physical parts? Presentation is just what it says, how are you going to organize and actually talk about what the problem was and how you took care of it. Think of it as content being the words, format being the music, and presentation being the actual song.

You need to address these three components in order to make a coherent presentation and breaking the task down into these components will make the overall task easier to accomplish. If you've never had the chance to make a presentation to the big bosses before, doing it this way will also cut down on your stress level.

I've always used some general guidelines to help me figure out the content of the presentation. The first thing I've always looked at is the point of the presentation. What message am I trying to get across? Am I pointing out a flaw in the system? Or am I just passing on information as to upcoming events that we need to plan for? In both cases, the first thing to do is use my boundaries and start at the beginning with a statement of the situation. It is much easier to relate a story by starting with a statement of the initial situation. Whether that be "we have a new customer coming in next month" or "this product we make has a lot of parts and a complicated assembly process", I start off with that statement of "this is how it is". The next thing I address is what the actual or potential problem is such as "this new customer wants us to make something we haven't done before" or "we have a high rejection rate on that product as a result of it being complicated". The last thing I want to address is "here is what the impact of that new customer's product" or "this is how I made that troublesome product easier to assemble". So the presentation breaks down to: Current Situation, Problem Statement, and Solutions. You don't want to put together a presentation in order of "here's what I did because this situation kept happening" because it is a lot easier to start a story at the beginning and not jump into it halfway through. *Your job is to start with the current situation so that you can lead your audience through the logical thought patterns that you followed, not jump into the middle of the story and appearing to be justifying why you did such and such.*

Think of the last time your partner asked "why is your car in the garage?". If you jump into the middle with "I needed to change the oil" there is a chance that you'll get a response of "so I had to lug all the groceries to the house in the rain - why couldn't you have waited until I got back from the store?". Then you are forced into justifying why changing the oil was a priority that couldn't wait. If you instead had said something like "I went out this morning, started my car and oil started spraying all over the driveway so I pushed it back into the garage to figure out what was going on. I found that the oil plug was not tightened down, so I took care of that but still had to change the oil before I could move the car out of the garage", in essence started with a description of the situation then went into the problem and corrective action you took, things probably would have been a bit smoother. (Who really thinks this way? But it does work.)

Figuring out the scope and point of the presentation sounds a bit like what I've said about setting goals, doesn't it? It should because you have been given a goal of making this presentation, so now you have to figure out the specifics of the goal and how to get there. Use the same method as I've outlined in the goals and planning chapter to determine the content of the presentation.

The next thing to work on is what words and pictures do you use to explain the content in an easy to explain, easy to understand way, i.e., the format. Some general rules to start with are:

Do not fill a page with words when a paragraph will do,

Do not use a paragraph when a sentence will do, and

Do not use a sentence when a phrase will do.

The reason behind this is the most crucial point of any presentation you make. Consider this question: What is the most important part of your presentation? Is it the words you use? Is it the charts and pictures that you include? Or is it your presentation of the material? This last item is the correct one; *it is your presentation of the material that counts the most.* If you do it correctly, people will remember you presenting the material more than they will remember what it is that you showed and that is what you want to achieve. So if the point of your presentation is centered around your verbal presentation of the material and not the words and pictures that you've put together, why are you spending any time putting together these words and pictures? Because like I said a couple paragraphs earlier, the content is the words that with the format or music combine to form the complete song which is your presentation. The words and music when put together make a song that depending on the way it is played (the way it is presented) may sound very different even though it is the same song. Think of "The Star Spangled Banner" and how it sounds so very differently when sung by different singers at all those football and baseball games, and also compare it to Jimi Hendrix' electric guitar version. It's the same words, the same music, but very very different sounding songs. That is the point behind your actual presentation of the material; your presentation of the material ties those words and music together to form either something very easy to listen to or something that grates on the listener's ears.

One other corollary point about this is that with using just significant words or phrases instead of whole sentences, you are not tied to what you may have originally intended when you used that phrase. You can take cues from your audience and make a judgment on the fly as to whether or not that phrase will inflame the audience, cause unneeded questions, or will pass unnoticed. Ok, for instance, you have included the phrase "certification pending" and the audience to that point has been asking a lot of questions around how late the estimated product is going to be. When you get to that phrase in your presentation, you can tailor some explanatory comments to the questions the audience has been asking to that point; you're not tying yourself to the written word. By using phrases instead of sentences or paragraphs you are allowing yourself greater leeway in what you actually say.

The whole point of using phrases (or 'bullets') is that you are only using the written word as an outline for what you are actually saying. The point is that you are the person making the presentation and these words being projected on a screen are just placeholders for what you are going to talk about. So you don't want the audience to be spending time actually reading the words you are displaying, you want them listening to you instead. If you put too many words on the screen, part of what you are saying is going to be ignored while the audience reads the words.

It's a similar story with graphics such as pictures, diagrams, and charts. If you display a chart with lots of bright colors and multiple lines zigzagging their way across the field, or a picture with several arrows pointing to various parts of the picture, people are going to spend time looking at the graphic trying to figure it out, and not paying attention to you.

Ok, go back to that last magic show or standup comedian that you went to see. At any given time, was your attention not focused on the magician or comedian? No, the magician or comedian had your attention for at least 95% of the show, and that's the effect that you are striving for when doing a presentation. You can use charts or pictures to talk about, but don't make them overly busy; just label or show what you are talking about and nothing else. If you clutter your graphics, there will always be at least one person out there that's going to ask you a question about something completely foreign to what you are talking about. If you are showing charts of trends or data aggregation, make them as simple as you can otherwise the audience will be asking questions such as "what's the time scale on that?" or "are you going to talk about those other data categories?". You want the audience to follow what you are saying and you don't need the distraction of letting them go down various bunny trails because you will have some difficulty getting your presentation back on track.

You have an outline of what points you want to go through and now you need to put them together into a coherent presentation. Walk through the presentation points and begin adding comments or clarification of what those points are. Once you've done this, you have your presentation in draft form. Now talk your way through it, speaking out loud. You will find points where the topic doesn't flow easily from one point to the next, other points where there isn't enough clarification of what you're saying, and more points where you find yourself running off the main topic. So it's time to start editing by adding in that clarification that was missing, deleting those points that stray from the topic and don't add significant value, and by adding in information where natural questions might come up.

Read through the latest version one more time and if you've put it together according to my guidelines, you'll find it flows naturally and more importantly makes sense. It should also feel comfortable as you practice talking your way through the presentation. Remember that if you've done your homework you will be knowledgeable of all the parts of the presentation. There are not many things that will make you look like you don't know what you're talking about more than being asked a specific question in the middle of your presentation and being forced to say "I don't know".

By now you have your close to final presentation put together and you're feeling fairly comfortable with it. It is time to work on your actual presentation of the material and the only way to do that is to practice, practice, and practice some more. Here are some general guidelines to keep in mind.

The most successful presenters out there:

Hold your attention and only let you see what they want you to see,

Can do a two-hour presentation with only two or three slides with no more than a half-dozen words on each (think of those hour-long television 'infomercials' on public television that tell you how to lose weight or how to be a better person),

Never waste an opportunity to show you they are in charge of their presentation,

Act like they want to be there and don't pout or grumble about having to take time out of their busy schedule to do this presentation,

Realize that they have been invited to make their presentation and don't disrespect the audience by turning their back on them to read what is on the slide, rather they face the audience as much as possible during their presentation,

Is the person with the most knowledge about their presentation in the room and displays it by being able to field questions about their topic, and

Anticipates and answers questions before they are asked.

The net result of keeping the above guidelines in mind is that you will appear calm, knowledgeable, and in control when you make your presentation. In case you haven't realized it yet, I am steering you towards the ultimate goal for making a successful presentation which is:

The actual written or viewed presentation does not matter as much as your presentation of the material, and by making a successful presentation you are convincing the boss that you know what you are doing and that in similar matters in the future you can be trusted to handle the situation without asking the boss for permission or approval. But beware of being too cocky because the big bosses probably know more than you do and if you can't lead them into agreement with you through your presentation of the situation and material, you will never get a second chance to convince them that you can be trusted.

So there is a lot more at stake in making a presentation than just relating information to the boss. By making a successful presentation you are making the case that you deserve the boss's respect and trust. You are not going to be a success in the office without these two things. With the boss's respect and trust, you will be given more leeway in how you accomplish your assignments and you will correspondingly be eligible for bigger and better assignments as well as promotions and raises.

Eventually during this or future presentations you will run up against a heckler. They could be the sniper who makes side comments in a loud whisper so that others can clearly hear it, or it could be the know-it-all that openly questions your knowledge on the presentation you're making. There are others but these are usually the main two that you run up against. To manage the sniper, sooner or later you're going to have to confront them and the sooner the better otherwise doubts will be raised by the general audience about whether you really do know what you're talking about. I don't mean that you have to snarl at them and tell them to shut their mouth because that will provoke others in the audience. Probably the best way to handle them is to repeat as much of what they've just said as you've heard and politely ask them if they want to elaborate on their comment now, or can the two of you discuss it after your presentation is done. This puts them on the spot and 99 times out of a hundred they will wilt and not make any more comments, allowing you to continue with your presentation. To work with the know-it-all, you take a similar stance with them but limit the options to just talking about it privately after your presentation is done. I've used "yes, that's an interesting point but I think you'll find I've covered that later in this presentation, but if you still want to discuss it lets meet after I'm done". You don't want to relinquish your temporary position of authority as presenter because the rest of your presentation will descend into chaos if you don't cut the hecklers off with the promise to talk about it later. You're also showing that you are reasonable and willing to discuss the matter whereas you are putting the heckler into the position of 'bad guy' who is interrupting this important presentation.

An important point to keep in mind is that if one of the top managers or the top manager in the meeting starts questioning you, stop and answer their questions. Give them a short answer and promise to talk more details after the presentation is over but give them some kind of answer right up front. They are the people that invited you to the meeting so they have a right to control at least a part of your presentation. Never go out on a limb and say something that isn't true or make up an answer. You will be found out sooner or later and all that work you put into being a success will be completely erased because now you will be known as a liar.

A different situation can arise where someone in the audience gets angry at what you're talking about. Try again with deferring to after your presentation is done but if that doesn't work then appeal to the top manager in the room to control the angry person. If the top manager in the room gets angry, stop what you're talking about and get them to give you the specifics of what they are angry about, then either admit that you hadn't considered that before, or try to salvage the rest of your presentation by saying the answer to their comments may be in later parts of your presentation. I had one infamous presentation to a fourth level manager and staff about budgets where the manager got really po-d at what I was saying. I did not make it off the first slide I was showing where I had the initial budget allocation that I anticipated. The manager asked me "and if I tell you that I was just told that our budget was being cut 20%, what does that do to your figures?". I responded with "well, if the budget is cut" and he cut me off and said "I just told you the budget was cut so there is no if about it". I didn't listen well enough and came back with "ok, so if the budget is cut" and he cut me off one more time and yelled "I just told you it was cut g-damn it so what the f-are you saying about if?". I hadn't been in this situation before so without thinking I said "if the..." and got no further when he starting yelling at me with a lot more colorful language than I thought he had imagination for and ended by ordering me out of the room and not to come back until I got the f-ing message. He even personally got up and slammed the conference room door behind me. Talk about not wanting to ever go back in there again...! A few days later I finally summoned up the courage to go to him again and while he was still a bit surly, he accepted what I showed him, then told me something very important which was "next time listen to what I say". So when the boss says something, pay attention.

Finally (finally!), unless you are an accomplished presenter, make an effort to keep your arms at your side during your presentation. And don't put your hands in your pants pockets while making your presentation. It will put you into an awkward posture and as a result, you will look awkward and people will start questioning your abilities. Use body language to your advantage; appear relaxed and your audience will relax because you look like you know what you're doing. As for making gestures with your hands, I remember attending one presentation where the person held their 18-ounce paper coffee cup while doing their presentation. Needless to say, at one point they got a bit animated and started flailing their arms around. I can still remember the panicked looks on some of the audience when the contents of the cup sprayed around the room. The lesson to be learned from this is only use your arms and hands to point to specific parts of the slides being shown or to make motions that correspond to what you are saying.

Summary point:

Your presentations should be organized around what the situation is or was, what problems may occur or have occurred, and finally what you have done to make sure everything is ok. Split up your presentation preparation into content or what you are going to talk about, format or what the presentation is going to look like and how it will flow, and finally presentation or how you will walk the audience through the presentation. Use succinct phrases and modest graphics throughout your presentation so as to keep your audience's attention focused on you. Practice your presentation over and over again so that you know exactly what you are going to say to amplify the phrases in the presentation and to be able to answer any questions that come up during the presentation. Research the subject thoroughly so that you have additional knowledge that you can bring up during the presentation if needed to answer questions. Keep cool and calm during the presentation and defuse hecklers by offering to discuss their points after you have completed your presentation. Use your presentation as a way of garnering the trust of management and convince them that you know what you are doing and can successfully handle similar situations in the future without management's express permission or authority.

Dealing with anchors, snipers, and saboteurs or, "were you born an a-hole?"

I previously went through a bunch of stereotypical personalities that you'll be dealing with in any given work environment. Most of them can be worked with most of the time and I've given you some tips on how to make working with them a bit more productive. Now I'm going to go through some personalities that are almost always toxic and will bring down your career if you let them. These are not your general workers; these are a set by themselves. They don't want to be working, don't want to try and make something of their career other than to get to the top as soon as they can, are sour on life in general, and most importantly usually like to cause others the same pain they are feeling internally. You may find yourself working with them at some time or another and about the best you can do is to avoid working with them. If you must work with them, be patient, be tolerant, but don't pay that much attention to them. Listen to them if you must but don't let their bad attitude bring yours down also.

So the "Anchor" is that person that drags their feet at everything. They delay doing anything as long as possible. When they do start doing something, they move so slowly that eventually someone else picks up the slack, which is what the anchor wanted all along. They don't want to work, they just want that paycheck and if they can stay under the radar by having other people do their work, so be it. They fiddle around all day looking like they are working but they don't produce anything. I remember one person that used to work for me. He looked busy all day long but when I checked the monthly production reports, he was at the bottom of the list with about one-tenth the product that an average worker produced. So after three months of being at the bottom of the list, I sat him down privately and asked if he was having problems understanding the job, or with the mechanics of the job, or what? He responded with comments about getting used to the job and this and that and really didn't have an intelligent answer. I put him on notice that he appeared to have all the training necessary as well as experience in related assignments and if he didn't start producing at a higher rate then I might have to have a more formal conversation with him. He promised to do better and sure enough, the next month's report showed him firmly in the middle of the group in terms of quantity and quality. We had another conversation at that time and I praised him for applying himself and told him to keep up the good work. He responded by saying he had found a new job at a different company and would be leaving in two weeks because our job was 'too draining' on him (I still remember that conversation). After he left, three of my leads came separately to tell me that it was a real relief that the anchor was gone because he was dragging the morale of everyone else down. Other people were struggling to get their own assignments done and resented having to pick up the slack from the anchor's workload while he just sat there and whiled away the day doing something, but nobody could ever figure out what that something was.

"Snipers" and "Saboteurs" are proactive parts of the workforce in that they actively work at cutting down other people's accomplishments. Snipers generally do it while and after other people are working specific assignments. Saboteurs do it before and during when other people are working. Snipers can sound friendly (like The Jokester) in that they will add comments to the end of other people's conversations such as when one person starts a conversation with "I was walking the dog yesterday" and the sniper chimes in with "I didn't know you were coordinated enough to walk" which will probably get some laughs from the immediate group. This sounds pretty innocuous by itself but if you listen to the general tone of repeated comments like this from the sniper, you'll see that there is a bit of a mean streak to them. They're good at chipping away at other people's reputations because they think it makes them better (to raise yourself, lower the others). Saboteurs are very similar except they may go the extra mile and start spreading rumors about someone else, and almost always bad rumors. Here's an example conversation: "did you see Joe this morning, he doesn't look too good" and the saboteur might say "yeah I heard somewhere that he likes his beer" thus implying that 'Joe' has a drinking problem. This is plain mean and it's what the saboteur does best. Both the sniper and the saboteur like to do this because they are inwardly afraid that they're not good enough, so bringing others down levels the playing field. Most of the time, they also enjoy doing it. There's not much you can do about them except don't let yourself get down to their level and stay out of their path. If they get really abusive, report them to management.

"The Fluffer" is very similar to The Lord of the Manor in that they don't really do a whole lot and like to tell other people how important their job is. The small difference is that the fluffer is also a suck-up to anyone in authority (look up 'fluffer' on the internet and you'll get a better idea of what they're really good at). They like to show how close they are to the boss by repeating any and all phrases that the boss tends to use a lot. If the boss is fond of saying things like "turd in the punchbowl", then you can count on the fluffer to use the exact same phrase, even if they don't really understand it, what context to use it in, or what it the boss meant when they used it. The best way to get around this person is to listen to what they say and when they walk away, promptly forget what they said because whatever it was, it doesn't mean a whole lot. They are of little use to the organization because they really don't know what the heck they're talking about, but watch out and don't openly ridicule them because in addition to everything else, they are tattle-tales and will try to get you into trouble with the boss just so they can get closer to the boss. They are usually pleasant people but they are toxic if you hang around with them because sooner or later they will stab you in the back, if they can get away with it.

Also worth mentioning is a close cousin of The Rulebook which I'll call "What-Rule". This person is like a cross between the Used Car Salesman and the Lord of the Manor in that they're impatient, don't do a whole lot, yet know the rules that govern the workplace. The problem is that they don't think that rules apply to them and almost dare people to report them for ignoring the workplace guidelines. You've met these people on the road; they're the ones driving 45 mph in a 30 mph zone, they use the middle turn lane on a two lane road to cut you off only to make a right turn at the next street, and they take two spaces when they park. The simple reason they do this and other aggravating things is that they believe the rules don't apply to them, usually because they were either pampered or ignored by their parents while they were growing up. They tend to have meteoric careers in which they can very quickly ascend the management ladder but when their real capabilities are tested and found lacking, they get shunted to some out of the way place with an important sounding title but little else. My advice is to just stay away from these people. They are probably the most self-absorbed egotistical and useless people that you will meet in the workplace. I say stay away because even though they may be friendly, easy to talk to, and relatively intelligent, they don't really care about developing a relationship with anyone other than the next higher sponsor that can give them a boost up the ladder. You'll find that most managers with a what-rule working for them will spend some effort in getting rid of the what-rule people because they generally have a negative effect on the rest of the group. This person is also accomplished at stealing other people's ideas. I remember one time when I was working on a team to solve a problem and we came up with a solution that looked like it would work. We put together a proposal and went to the manager with it. The manager surprised us with "I already gave the green light to that solution, didn't [x] tell you that?". It seems that our resident what-rule person had already gone to the manager and presented the solution as his own. Take care when working with this type of personality because they are only in the game to make themselves look good.

Writing about these personalities is getting me down so I'll finish off with the person that is just the general a-hole. Most of them are just mean self-centered people. I remember hearing a song with the refrain "were you born an a-hole or did you just turn out that way" and I could ask that about more than a couple people I've run into over the years. I also can't confine this personality to just the workplace. The last time you were in the checkout line at the store and some person tried to butt in line ahead of you, didn't you at least think (if not openly say) "what an a-hole"? In the workplace, this is the person that grabs your pen off your desk and when you ask for it back they tell you to go to the supply cabinet for a new one. They pour the last of the coffee from the maker and then walk away without making a new pot, or better yet they see that the coffee pot is empty, walk away, and wait for someone else to make a new pot. They are the ones that cause you to label your lunch in the refrigerator and then they'll still take it while you're not looking. I was eating my cinnamon raisin bagel and an apple for lunch one day and this person I'd never met before walked by, stopped, then came back to tell me that I shouldn't be eating the bagel because "they'll kill you sooner or later" – thank you your a-holiness. The somewhat dim person in the desk next to mine saw me eating a granola bar and started expounding on how gluten was the cause of all my ills including waking up in the morning with a stuffed nose (I happen to have hay fever) – what an a-hole. Everybody can be one at one time or another but these people are maddening with their constant a-holiness. They're also the person that throws stuff on the floor at their workstation then walks away leaving someone else to clean it up. Most people will do something like this every now and then because they're not paying attention but the real a-holes of the workplace do this day in and day out. What do you do with these people? About the only thing you can do is to report them to management and hope for the best. The best circumstance is when you catch them stealing something because that is usually a dismissible offence in most workplaces. Other than that, about the only thing that can be done is to get the rest of the people in the workplace to watch and complain about them. The failing that these a-holes have is that they don't make provision for ticking off everyone and if your workgroup can show some unity you may be able to get some changes made, either in their work attitude or in getting assistance from management in dealing with them.

Summary point:

You will meet and have to work with people that are just toxic to be around sooner or later. The best way to work with these people is to be cordial but to stay out of their way and keep off their radar, i.e., avoid them. They bring the general morale of the workplace down and they don't really accomplish a whole lot. Just stay away.

Image Does Count

Yeah yeah, we all know that 'office casual' or 'business casual' is the way to dress for your job, but think about what you wear to your business before you leave home in the morning. Dressing appropriately for your job should become second nature after a while. If you work in a machine shop, you're going to get dirty so you don't want to show up at work in a tuxedo. If you're working in a tire store or a restaurant, chances are you have a uniform or similar item you should wear. If you're working in an office, gauge the dress code from what you see others wearing and wear appropriate attire so that you don't stick out on the high end or low end of the spectrum. I worked in an office over a manufacturing shop at one time and we had this one person that routinely wore flowered shorts, flip-flops, and patterned t-shirt to work probably nine months out of the year. Number one consideration I always thought of when I saw this "surfer dude" walking by was safety. The shop below us worked with adhesives, bolts and screws, heat guns, lubricants, chemical cleaners, very heavy items, and other things that were best touched only with gloves and here was this guy walking around with lots of exposed flesh. He claimed he never had to walk through the shop so that was why he could wear what he did. Ok, so he wasn't violating any safety rules but he was sure violating dress rules as far as I was concerned.

Think about how you look for your workplace. If you are working the perfume and makeup counter at the store in the mall, do you want to look like you just got out of bed after an all-nighter at the local bar? If you go to work looking like that you will be extremely lucky if anyone buys any of the products you're trying to sell. If you were to go to the local funeral home to make arrangements for your mother's unexpected death, do you want to talk to someone who looks like the surfer dude I described above?

Appearance and manner of dress do make a difference in your workplace. If you look the part, people's first impression of you will be favorable. The old axiom is "you never get a second chance to make a first impression" and it is very true, no matter what anyone says. I don't care if you are the most liberal minded, accepting person on earth; there will be occasions where that first impression will cause either a favorable or unfavorable reaction in you.

If you are walking down a busy downtown street and see a person in ragged clothes, obviously unwashed, and unruly hair all over the place, you make the connection that this is most likely a homeless person which may inspire good or bad thoughts in you. If you are walking down that same street at night and see a large male walking towards you with a scowl on their face and their hands bunched into fists, you most likely will get the idea that you'd better move towards the side of the sidewalk because this could be a troublesome person.

It is the same at your workplace. If you look like you belong there, look collected, look like you made an effort to look like your job means something to you, people will trust you and your judgement more. Even if you're a grease monkey in the local garage you want to look like you care about the details of the job because that inspires trust and confidence in your work. If you had your choice of people to paint the inside of your house, all other things being equal would you choose the person in ragged shorts, t-shirt, and sandals or would you choose the person in the coveralls that have their name stenciled on them? Do you want to go to your doctor's office and be examined by a person in shorts and a Hawaiian shirt or someone who is wearing perhaps that obnoxious white lab coat? Would you buy something from a butcher than has dirty fingernails? What inspires trust in you more when you meet someone professionally for at least the first time?

Dressing for the job is one thing that will make others trust you and over time that trust will become respect. So we used to have those outliers that didn't care about the image they presented, from surfer dude to what some would refer to as 'hot mamas', those younger women that wore the same thing to the office that they would wear when going clubbing at night. That guy and those women didn't put much thought into what others thought about them, *which is ok by me*, but when that image impression cuts into your credibility, you lose.

Dressing for your work doesn't make you any better than others in the workplace, but it could make you look worse. The vast majority of people nowadays come to work in some variation of blue jeans or other casual pants, and that is fine. So why would anyone want to over- or under-dress and stick out like a sore thumb is beyond me.

The goal you are striving for is to inspire trust and respect from your co-workers and your managers and if you come in looking like you just spent a month in a refugee camp you are not going to inspire much more than "ick!". You have to make the impression that you care about your job and that you pay attention to the details. Do you want to do a tire rotation job and have the customer doubt whether you really tightened all those lug nuts just because you look like a mess? Sure, we all know some of those workers that look like hell all the time but are absolutely gifted at what they do but try to think back to when you first met them and what your initial thought was – don't lie, there was a bit of doubt there until you started talking to them and found out they knew a whole bunch more than you. *Looks can be deceiving and it will only take time to really demonstrate your abilities, but it is much better and easier to be working to confirm what people first thought about you than working to change their first opinions.*

Summary point:

Look like you care about your work and you will inspire confidence in your abilities. Dress appropriately for your work and pay attention to details. *Pay attention to the small details or people won't believe you paid attention to any details.*

Dealing with office politics

This is going to be the shortest chapter of all, which should give you a clue as to how important this topic is, i.e., not that much.

Sooner or later you're going to run into 'office politics', those unwritten 'rules' about who really runs the place, which people to avoid, what words or phrases you should never use, who tattles on everyone else, what the office's real agenda is, who is making time with that other person over there, etc. It will be a hopeless mish-mash of things to remember, things to avoid, ways to act or dress, and other things vaguely important or really forgettable.

Basically, office politics to pay attention to are a collection of what 'the boss' likes and dislikes added to the workings of the various 'cliques' that are in just about every office. Ask about how the workplace works and you'll get replies along the lines of "those two really run this place", "don't hang around with him too much because he's on the sh-t list and you don't want to get any of the stink on you", and other gems that can be worthwhile to at least listen to even if you end up not paying that much attention to them.

The only things you really want to pay attention to are what the boss likes or dislikes. If the boss doesn't like practical jokes, for pete's sake don't pull any. If the boss pays a lot of attention to people being at their workstations during work hours, by all means be there. If the boss likes facts and figures, make sure you have them at hand.

The rest of the "do's and don'ts" of the office can be useful for not stepping on other people's toes, but really, they aren't that important. The most important things to remember are those things that emanate from the boss either directly or indirectly. There will be those people that "have the boss's ear" that you may want to get to know, but what those people may say still comes indirectly from the boss.

The rest of office politics is going to be based in gossip, like who is seeing who outside the workplace, and other interesting yet pretty irrelevant information. Don't pay that much attention to any of it unless it comes directly or indirectly from the boss. A lot of it is started by people that are unhappy with their work and are just looking to start trouble for someone else, namely you. Don't get sucked into playing the game because as with any game, there are winners and losers and you sure as heck don't want to be on the short end of the stick at the end of the day.

Summary point:

Remember the golden rule of the workplace: Focus on the situation, problem, or work to be accomplished and keep the personalities and office politics out of the picture.

Do I leave or stick it out?

So there comes a time in everyone's career where they ask themselves "do I go look for another job or do I stick it out here for at least another couple years?". The reason why this question comes up is because you're feeling bored with the assignments, you don't really care for who you're working with, you don't get along with your manager too well, or you know of a different job that you think would suit you better or at least sounds more like what you've really wanted to do. There may also be outside influences on you such as a partner that wants to move somewhere else, etc., but I'll just stick with what you're feeling internally.

Look at what you're presently doing for work. Now look back at the different chapters up to now. Start off by asking yourself why am I working? You should know the answer to that question by now. If you're working to pay the bills or to make a decent life for your children, then you'll be needing to look a little deeper into why you are working this specific job. We'll look at if you are working to make a difference a little later.

So the main reason why you are working is to raise some cash to pay the bills associated with your style of life or to provide a good home for the children. That doesn't automatically mean that you enjoy your work, but if you do then you shouldn't be asking yourself if you need to find a new job. If you enjoy your present job and it pays all the bills and feeds the kids, then there is no reason to change jobs. Ah but that other job that you were looking at in Sunday's want ads pays more. And if you get paid more you can afford a better lifestyle, a newer car, a bigger house for the children, a college fund, etc. So in reality, there is another factor to add in to the equation along with job satisfaction and paying the bills. *It's the desire to get ahead.* If all you want to do is stay in one spot and live a comfortable life in your present job that pays enough and gives you satisfaction, then there is no need to even ask whether or not you should consider moving to a different job.

The majority of people out there want more, more of anything and more of everything. They want to afford that newer car now; they want that bigger house now; and they want that college fund now. However, in order to pay for those items, something else has to be squeezed. It's like a balloon where if you want to expand one area you squeeze the opposite end. So it is in life. If you want that bigger house so the kids all have their own bedrooms, then you'll have to squeeze somewhere else. Whether that means cutting back on the take-out dinners multiple times per week or putting up with that clunker of a car for another year but something is going to have to give. If there is no other area to squeeze then you'll have to get a bigger balloon, i.e., find a higher paying job so the entire balloon is bigger.

Now, if the reason why you are working is to make a difference, you shouldn't be feeling empty at this point, unless you are not in the right job. You will know that you are not in the right job because you will not feel like you are not making a difference. The job is not fulfilling one of your key needs in life. If you do go looking for another job because of this, you'll have to start back with the basic question of why you are working and go from there, again. But at least this time you will know what doesn't work for you, which is a lot more information than you had when you initially started working.

Now that you've gone through why you are working you'll have to go back to your goals in life and review them to see if they are still valid goals. If they are, then you need to look at your plans for achieving your goals. Have you strayed from the plan, or have you reached a dead end? If your goals are still desirable, then are your plans still workable or is there something that wasn't taken into account when you made your plans? You wanted to be that airline pilot and took the necessary classes then signed up for pilot's school and found that you have a fear of heights? That's an unplanned for event that definitely calls for a rethinking of your goals and corresponding plans. Or you always wanted to be a middle to upper level manager in your company, but along the way through your promotions you met a person, got married, and now have children who demand time, time that you initially thought you were going to devote to your managerial responsibilities. That situation may take some thinking and reflecting on whether or not you want to continue to pursue that goal, and if so, then definitely you'll want to make some mid-course changes to your action plans so that you can still achieve your goal yet also meet your familial responsibilities.

Or are you on track with your plans but plan B has a slightly different path to the same goal and plan A is getting difficult to carry through? You've run up against a roadblock that you just can't budge so maybe it's time to figure a different way to your goal.

Whatever the case, you'll have to sit down and spend a little time on whether you really want to leave your current job because it doesn't satisfy some inner need, or it doesn't get you closer to your life goal, or just because it doesn't satisfy why you are working.

Whatever you do, do not give your current assignment the short end of the stick. Upon examination, you may find that you really do like your current job but it's something else that you're not quite satisfied with. It may be someone else in the workplace annoys you, it may be the hour-long commute twice a day, or it may be something as simple as your physical workplace is filthy. The job assignment is what you want but it's the intangible other things associated with it that make you unhappy or unsatisfied.

And it could just as easily be part of your personality that is driving you to consider other jobs. You feel this restlessness inside you that builds from week to week, month to month. That's most likely boredom you're feeling. Your mental self knows that you've made your mark in this place and it is time to move on and learn something different and achieve something new.

Whatever the case, in order to decide whether it's time to move on or to stay put for another couple years, that decision and the thought process leading up to it are going to be for the most part, your decision only. Yes, you may run into a situation where your parent or other close relative has to go into a managed care facility and therefore you need to be closer to them in case something happens. Even in these cases, there are still other ways around the situation. You may feel that you are obligated to put your life aside in order to assist someone else but there are ways that you can maintain most if not all of your current life by bringing those people to you instead of moving to their side. I got wanderlust one time after about 8 years in one job and went to another much smaller company where I could get a similar position. After interviewing with them and walking around their business I was left with the impression that although I could make more money, it was going to be a much tougher job since I would be the only person in my job category and therefore I would have to be on-call for at least two shifts a day. That didn't sit well with me since I like to leave work behind when I get home. Plus, their workplace was operating on a shoestring budget to maximize profits and as a result was downright filthy. I decided that my current job at the time was a lot more secure (that other company actually went out of business two years later) and fit my requirements a lot better so I turned down their offer. On the other hand, I have a relative that moved between companies every 4 or 5 years because he got bored and wanted bigger and better jobs. I am not saying that one or the other philosophy was better or worse, just that they were different which is natural given that we are all different people.

You have to make that decision whether or not the grass is greener on the other side. You have to take a look at why you are currently working this job and what might be different and better with a different job. Weigh the pros and cons and make a decision, and for your own peace of mind don't ever revisit that decision later on because it will drive you crazy. It's like investing in the stock market; if I would have bought this company's stock ten years ago when I first heard of it I'd be a millionaire today. That kind of second-guessing yourself will cause you to lose faith in yourself and your capabilities. If you decide not to take that other job, is there something in the back of your head that's saying "don't do this" and setting off a warning bell? If there is, that new job is not going to be what you think because you're trying to sell yourself that the new job is more than what it is. I'm not saying that moving to a new job isn't naturally going to cause some jitters, but there is that something else that is telling you not to do it because it doesn't quite fit in with what you really want. There are many people out there that will accept jobs that really don't fit their bill because they know that it will only be an interim step to something else which is much more desirable. Ok, but if that ultimate job doesn't materialize then it is time to go back to the drawing board and figure out just what you really do want. I used to work with a lot of contract (temporary) engineers at one time. Some of the younger people I worked with looked at these contractors and quit their jobs to go work contract because the job looked like it had the best combination of working conditions; high pay, freedom to move around the country at the drop of a hat, and no real allegiances to maintain. Within ten years, almost all of them were back working full-time for my company

72

because the stress of working in San Francisco for a couple months then being told they had to be in San Antonio in three days' time for the next assignment for a couple months, then someplace else for a couple months, as well as having no medical benefits, no investment plans, no retirement plans, etc. just got to be too much. There were a few that continued however, proving that everyone is different.

So if you're wondering whether or not it is time to move to a different job you need to look at what is causing that feeling. Is it truly you don't feel comfortable or satisfied with the job, or is there something else? Is it that smelly person that you have to deal with on a daily basis, you and your boss just don't get along really well, or you have a two hour commute each day to work, something is causing you to have these feelings of unease. Until you can figure out what is the driver behind those feelings you will never be able to justify to yourself moving to another job. If it's something simple as you need or want more money, then finding and securing that job that will give you more money will definitely salve your inner feelings. But many people just don't feel right in their job and they can't put a finger on it, relying instead on "I don't like working here". If you stick with that as a reason for job-hopping, you're rarely going to find a job that does make you happy and contented.

Summary point:

You must look at the reasons why you need to work and what your goals are in order to either stay where you are or find something else. Whatever you decide, don't second-guess your decision and fill your mind with "woulda, coulda, shoulda" because all that will do is cause ongoing mental anguish.

Now what are you going to do about your current job and your career?

Afterword

I've led you through a series of topics and steps to help you work more successfully and hopefully you've gained at least a couple ideas on how to be a success. Remember that *each person is different and what you want and need is different from your partner's, your neighbor's, your sibling's, and your offspring's needs and desires.* Outside circumstances combined with your own attributes and desires make it certain that the success the guy down the block has will be different than the success you achieve. Stop trying to be like successful people you know or see on the television because everyone is different and success means different things to different people. Is it important to you to have a new turbocharged car every year like your cousin? Is there some other way that you can show success other than with that specific material possession? I know a couple that get a new car every two to three years because they don't like to pay for heavy maintenance, but they have almost no equity in their home and very little money in the bank. On the other hand, I drive a 15-year-old car but have more than enough money in the bank to ensure a very comfortable retirement while the other guy probably has to continue working until he dies of old age. Success looks different to different people and *it's not what others think of you but what you think of yourself.*

So spend some time getting to know yourself because it will pay off in a more successful, more pleasant, and more pleasing life. And drum it into your mind that nothing comes without some effort on your part, and that nothing happens overnight – *patience is a virtue.*

Note for my readers: Please leave me a comment on my Amazon author page (https://www.amazon.com/W.L.W.-Borowiecki/e/B01IS3RIBE/ref=dp_byline_cont_ebooks_1) about what I've written, also take a look at more books that might interest you.

I'm always open to compliments, suggestions, general comments, 'constructive criticism", etc. Aggressive or obscene comments will usually give me a good laugh but not much more attention than that... I am not a condescending person; I'd much rather listen than speak so this is your chance to speak and for me to listen.

www.ingramcontent.com/pod-product-compliance
Lightning Source LLC
Chambersburg PA
CBHW071620170526
45166CB00003B/1121